Welcome to the Exam Kit

This isn't really a Book. (You've probably got more like a toolbox, or a First Aid kit. It's got loads of stuff in it: you take out what you need, when you need it. And you use it – to solve problems and get things done. That's the Exam Kit.

How does it work?

The Exam Kit identifies what you need to improve your exam performance.

- Signpost Questionnaires – to pinpoint weak areas, danger spots, and best options
- Check-up Checklists – to help you think things through

The Exam Kit offers tools, techniques and tips for revision and exams.

- Action Checklists – for sensible techniques and procedures that really work
- Templates – of timetables, worklists and note cards, for you to copy and use
- Toolbox pages – with ready made mnemonics and note forms to get you started
- Go for It! – questions and activities that actually get you doing the stuff!

The Exam Kit helps you stay human!

- Problem features – where we get to grips with your gripes
- People features – where we hear from examiners, students and celebs
- Get a Life! features – where we find there really *is* life after exams

How to use the Exam Kit

The Exam Kit is divided into ten Sections, covering different aspects of Revision and Exams. Within each Section are Units dealing with specific topics, situations and techniques. It's totally flexible, so you can use it in any way that suits you.

- Use our unique Signpost Questionnaires to identify exactly where you need help – and exactly where to find it!
- Dip into any Unit that looks interesting, and use the Unit-to-Unit links to follow up on related topics.
- Follow a 'strand' of Units, drawing together all the advice on a particular issue: starting late, or getting stressed...
- Tackle relevant Units for the stage of revision you're at (even After the Exam!)
- Start at the beginning and work through all relevant Units. (Fine – if you have time. But if you're just trying to put off 'real' revising, be warned: Exam Kit won't let you!)

START HERE
Contents list (sort of): page 6
Signpost Questionnaire: page 2 (Revision), or page 46 (Exams)

QUESTIONNAIRE

In the Exam Kit, we don't just want to give you 'good revision advice', we want to get *your* problems spotted – and solved. Try this quick quiz…

For each question, circle the letter of the answer that's closest to what you feel yourself.

1. Why *do* you think it's worth putting effort into revising?

   A It will refresh my memory, and get me into exam 'mode'.
   B I've got loads to catch up! Short-term memory – and bluff – will get me through.
   C I'll have answers ready: all I'll need is the questions to put them to.
   D I don't. (Dumb question.)

2. When did you (or when do you intend to) start your revision?

   A About 6–8 weeks before the exam.
   B About 3–4 weeks before the exam.
   C You what? It's 2 weeks before the exams now – and I haven't done anything!
   D Trick question, eh? I've been revising bit by bit all year. Naturally.

3. If you woke up and realised you were going to be late for an exam, what would you do?

   A Pass out. Throw up. (And get mum to say I was sick.)
   B Shout. Rush around. Get to the exam late and be completely rattled.
   C Get ready super-quick and do anything to get to the exam on time.
   D Just go in and start the exam late.

4. How long is it from now to your first exam?

   A Oh, months.
   B 3–8 weeks.
   C 1 week.
   D It's tomorrow! Aaaargh…

5. What sort of revision plan do you (intend to) use?

   A A timetable. What else?
   B I don't really make a plan – just a list of topics for the day.
   C Loads of different ones: I have to redo them anyway, when I fall behind…
   D You're kidding, right?

6. Which of the following best describes you? (More than one, if you like.)

   A I can usually tell how long a task will take me.
   B If I'm going shopping, I like to take a list of things I need to buy.
   C I use a diary/personal organiser/school timetable to 'keep track' of myself.
   D I tend to be late for things, and never finish tasks when I'm supposed to.

7. How long do you (intend to) spend on each revision 'session'?

   A As long as I can stay awake. (I've got so much to do!)
   B As long as I can stay awake. (There's always more I could be doing.)
   C A few hours.
   D A few hours – broken up into short chunks: say, half an hour.

QUESTIONNAIRE

Revision

8. What have you got on your work surface at this moment?

A What worksurface?
B Yes, yes, I know. I keep meaning to tidy it up. Don't hassle me now. I'm revising.
C Subject textbook, Study Text and notes. Pen and paper.
D Oh, *loads* of stuff: don't worry – I've got everything I could *possibly* need!

9. When *do* you most feel like giving up on an assignment/revision session?

A Before I've even started: I just can't face it!
B In the middle of a session: I get so bored!
C Towards the end of a day: I feel like I'm missing out on life!
D It's not that I *feel* like giving up: I just sort of get distracted...

10. What revision techniques do you (intend to) use regularly

A Mind-mapping, mnemonics, index-cards, past papers. The usual.
B Reading. Re-reading. Concentrating really hard. Muttering a lot...
C *Techniques*? Now you tell me?! I'll never learn them in time!
D I reduce my notes mainly – to lists or diagrams – and then test myself.

OVERALL

Which of the following revision 'types' sounds most like you? (We identified some of the answers each might have picked in the questionnaire, to help you decide.)

A You've been reviewing your classwork regularly all year, and by the time you reach Final Revision Phase (8 weeks), you've got everything neatly in a file-card system of diagrams and mnemonics. You've drawn up a detailed timetable for lots of revision and timed mock tests. After all, what's more important than that A* grade?

B You know your classnotes are in reasonable order, but you'll need 6 weeks of Final Revision to reduce them and review them with the exam in mind. You have a basic plan, which allows for some breaks and variety. You try to be flexible: some days are tougher than others. You want to do well – but you're trying to be sensible about it.

C You know there are a few gaps and muddles in your classnotes. And time is ticking away. Deep down, you know you ought to be more determined and more organised. Your short-term memory will have to come to the rescue: you tell yourself you can still do OK, with 3 or 4 weeks of all-out 'cramming'. How much sleep does a person need?

D You're losing it: you know you are. The exams are getting closer and you can't find anything, and you can't remember anything, and you know you should be well into your revision but you can just never seem to get down to work, and you just hate yourself, and – aargh!

E It really gets up your nose how everyone goes on about Exams and Revision. It's all a waste of time. Your classnotes? Best paper 'plane you ever made ...

QUESTIONNAIRE

Your score

If you answered...

Actually, you don't get a score. Sorry. But there are no 'right' or 'wrong' answers here: only answers that might say something useful about you and your revision approach.

Where to?
Try Unit(s)...

1. Your general approach to revision
A: You have a pretty healthy idea of what revision is for. Move on...
B: You're taking a lot of risks and may be putting yourself under
unnecessary pressure.   1.1
C: You're making a big mistake. Don't waste any more time thinking
this way.   1.1, 8.2
D: Oooh... *Major* Attitude Problem! Do you *want* to get past it?   2.1

2. The sensibleness (or not) of your revision campaign
A: You're on the right track: as long as you keep to your resolve.
Move on...
B: You'll be pushing it! Ideally, rethink your start date.   1.2
Or recognise that Time is Tight: adjust your revision accordingly.   2.4, 3.4, 6.1
C: Don't panic! You need to get things under control now.
First, work out why you've left it so late.   4.1
Next, make the most of your revision time.   2.4, 3.4, 6.1
D: You're too good to be true. But before you get too cocky...   2.3

3. How you feel and handle pressure
A: You really don't react well to pressure situations! Focus on
'healthy' revision.   2.2, 2.5
B: You tend to let pressure get to you. It will help to focus on
organised revision.   2.4, 6.1
C: You probably do your best work under pressure! Bear it in mind...   2.2, 2.3
D: You sound pretty laid back. Just check that you're still awake...   2.2, 2.3

4. Where you are in the revision phase
A: Check out the Exam Kit at your own pace. (But try not to become
a Swotaholic!)
B: If you're at the 8 week end: perfect. Carry on...
If you're at the 3 week end: check your pressure gauge...   6.1, 6.2
C: You're almost there: keep going – sensibly!   6.3
D: Don't panic.   6.4

5. Your approach to revision planning
A: Great. (As long as you really do use it...) Carry on...
B: Don't worry: your list is a perfectly good plan! Carry on...
C: You're not planning sensibly or realistically enough.   3.1, 3.4
D: No, we're serious. You must plan your revision. Start now.   3.1

6. The type of plan that might suit you
A: You'd probably be good with timetabling. Try it, if you haven't
already.   3.2
B: You're naturally a 'worklist' person. Go for it! For maximum
effectiveness...   3.3
C: You're naturally a timetabler. Go for it! For maximum effectiveness...   3.2
D: You're unlikely to get on with timetables. Try the alternative approach.   3.3

QUESTIONNAIRE

Your score

7. Sensible revision effort
A: You're not thinking straight. Desperation doesn't help...   2.4, 3.5
B: You're sounding like a Swotaholic. Beware burnout!   3.5
C: OK: you'll probably get away with it. But you're missing a trick...   3.5
D: You're on track. Stick with it!...

8. Revision organisation
A: You have a basic problem. You need to solve it now.   4.2
B: Sorry, but you're just giving yourself unnecessary hassles...   4.2
C: You're well on track. Carry on...
D: You've missed the point. (It's buried under the irrelevant junk on your desk...)   5.1

9. Getting – and keeping – yourself going
A: You have a problem getting down to work. Start by sorting out why.   4.1
B: You're not getting into revision. But it can be done!   5.2
C: You're just not suited to be a Swotaholic. Good! Lighten up a little...   3.5, 5.7
D: You're just going to have to kick start yourself!   4.3

10. Revision techniques
A: Yes, Super Swot, you know who you are...
B: You know how boring and pointless it is. Don't you?   5.2
C: Don't panic! Two basic tactics will make all the difference.   5.3, 5.4
D: You're fine. Why not just practise your 'scanning' techniques for some extra tips...   5.5, 5.6

OVERALL

A   We'll call you **SUPER SWOT**. We hardly even need to wish you luck. Just don't be a Swotaholic: keep an eye on your stress levels, get some rest before the exams – and go for it!

B   We'll call you **UNDER CONTROL**. Well done. You're doing a good job, and giving yourself your best chance of success. Still, you can make your revision even more efficient and effective. Check out some of our tips – and use them, if they're right for you. Good luck!

C   We'll call you **UNDER PRESSURE**. Basically, you've left yourself with a lot to do. You have to get a grip on yourself and your time. You haven't picked an Easy Way: you'll need more effective revision planning and technique than most. You can do it, though. Good luck!

D   We'll call you **GETTING DESPERATE**. You don't need to be told that you need help. But don't despair: (a) you are not alone, and (b) you *can* get yourself under control: starting with the Exam Kit! So chin up: you are now, officially, Getting Less Desperate! Good luck!

E   We'll have to call you **GAME OVER**. But you're wrong about this. Exams *do* matter – to you, and to those who care about you. And revision *can* make a difference to your grades. If you tell yourself you're going to fail, you will – but it'll be down to nobody but you. Is that the kind of 'being in control of your life' you want? Have the guts to go for it. Good luck!

Contents list (sort of...)

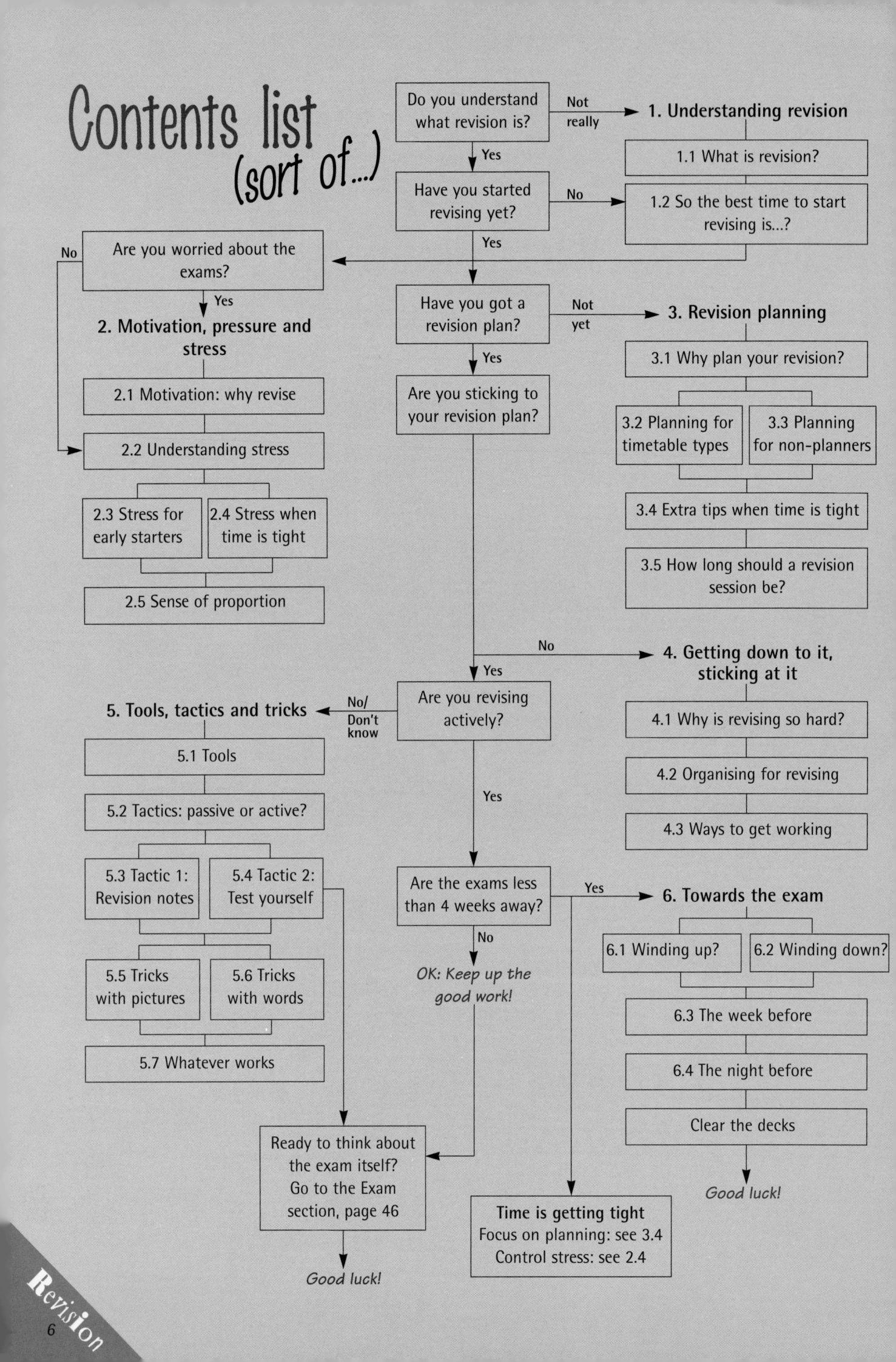

- Do you understand what revision is?
  - **Not really** → **1. Understanding revision**
    - 1.1 What is revision?
    - 1.2 So the best time to start revising is...?
  - **Yes** → Have you started revising yet?
    - **No** → 1.2 So the best time to start revising is...?
    - **Yes** → Have you got a revision plan?
      - **Not yet** → **3. Revision planning**
        - 3.1 Why plan your revision?
        - 3.2 Planning for timetable types
        - 3.3 Planning for non-planners
        - 3.4 Extra tips when time is tight
        - 3.5 How long should a revision session be?
      - **Yes** → Are you sticking to your revision plan?
        - **No** → **4. Getting down to it, sticking at it**
          - 4.1 Why is revising so hard?
          - 4.2 Organising for revising
          - 4.3 Ways to get working
        - **Yes** → Are you revising actively?
          - **No/Don't know** → **5. Tools, tactics and tricks**
            - 5.1 Tools
            - 5.2 Tactics: passive or active?
            - 5.3 Tactic 1: Revision notes
            - 5.4 Tactic 2: Test yourself
            - 5.5 Tricks with pictures
            - 5.6 Tricks with words
            - 5.7 Whatever works
          - **Yes** → Are the exams less than 4 weeks away?
            - **Yes** → **6. Towards the exam**
              - 6.1 Winding up?
              - 6.2 Winding down?
              - 6.3 The week before
              - 6.4 The night before
              - Clear the decks
              - *Good luck!*
            - **No** → OK: Keep up the good work!

- Are you worried about the exams?
  - **No** → (loop back)
  - **Yes** → **2. Motivation, pressure and stress**
    - 2.1 Motivation: why revise
    - 2.2 Understanding stress
    - 2.3 Stress for early starters
    - 2.4 Stress when time is tight
    - 2.5 Sense of proportion

Ready to think about the exam itself? Go to the Exam section, page 46

Good luck!

Time is getting tight
Focus on planning: see 3.4
Control stress: see 2.4

1 UNDERSTANDING REVISION

1.1 What is revision?

Revision is whatever you make it. But let's get clear (a) what you're trying to achieve, and (b) what revision can do for you.

1 → Revision is **FIXING IN YOUR MEMORY** things that you know.

Like a computer, your memory holds information in store for future reference. Revision is like 'saving' information on a disk. If you've done your coursework, the 'input' and the 'processing' of the data has already happened: you have learned and understood the topic. But the knowledge needs to be stored in your memory, so it can be 'called up' later.

2 → Revision is **LEARNING TO UNLOCK YOUR MEMORY** in the exam.

All the information stored in a computer can't be 'on screen' all the time. When you want a piece of data, you have to call it up: you need a menu or code to 'access' the information. Your mind works in the same way. Revision gives you memory prompters which can be used to bring what you know into your mind when you need it – in the exam room!

3 → Revision is **LEARNING TO ADAPT WHAT YOU KNOW** to an exam.

If your computer printed out long lists of numbers, when you asked for a graph, you'd be pretty annoyed. That's how examiners feel when you don't answer their questions! Revision is a chance to think about how you would select and use the things you know, to answer specific exam questions – in the style required and in the time available.

So revision isn't...?
- It's NOT trying to learn lots of new topics
- It's NOT trying to do two years' work in two weeks
- It's NOT trying to memorise notes or essays to reproduce in the exam

RE-VISION = SEEING AGAIN

Let's get this straight.

If you haven't already covered and understood a topic, you won't be revising: you'll be *learning*. This is harder to do on your own, and it takes longer.

→ Talk to a teacher – as in, NOW! – about any topics you think you've missed or misunderstood. (They may or may not be important: it's always worth asking...)

→ If you do have some catching up to do, allow for extra time in your revision plan.

action → Unit 3.4 will help.

Top tip

Clear the decks for revision as early in your course as you can! At the end of each week, review your class notes and handouts on all the week's topics. Check that they're

- Complete
- Correct
- Clear

Get any problems or gaps sorted out, as soon as you can. Your Final Revision Phase is for Final Revision!

UNDERSTANDING REVISION

1.2 So the best time to start revising is...?

**Never mind when your first *exam* is.
The best time to start *revising* is TODAY.**

6–8 WEEKS: 'INTENSIVE' and 'SENSIBLE'

- **If it's the beginning of your course: terrific!**

  Why not review some of your notes from time to time throughout the year? You don't have to be too heavy about it: just pick a topic, and see whether it 'rings a bell'. That shouldn't be too painful – and it all adds up!

- **If it's 6–8 weeks before the first exam: great!**

  This is pretty much the IDEAL TIME to be starting an intensive – and sensible – Final Revision Phase.

- **If it's 3–4 weeks before the first exam: OK...**

  If you haven't started yet, your Final Revision Phase is going to be intensive. Really intensive. But don't panic. It can still be sensible as well – provided you get moving NOW. Cramming is not the Easy Option: you'll need to be a lot more hardworking and efficient – from now on – than those who started work weeks ago... But you can do it!

- **If it's less than 2 weeks before the first exam: Panic!**

  Only kidding. You can still do it – if you're up for it. But if you really haven't started revising yet, there's a problem somewhere. If you don't know what it is, Unit 4.1 is a good place to start. Get it sorted...

There's so much you can do to boost your confidence – and your grades! If you can start early, and spread the workload over a longer period, you'll be able to:

- accomplish more
- use sensible techniques which maximise your memory – with less strain on your brain
- fit in more rest, relaxation and recreation (the Real Three Rs)
- avoid unnecessary pressure and stress

UNDERSTANDING REVISION

People

Will Carling
Pretty much Under Control, we reckon...

"There were people who always had everything worked out – and I was never one of those... but it's the same thing that makes you go out training when it's pouring with rain on a Thursday evening, or whatever. You think about what it is you want to do ultimately. You know you'll have to do a certain amount of work to get there. So you think: 'yeah, right, get on with it'."

"I wasn't someone who rose to exams. I dreaded them. I was what you'd call 'Last-minute Lucy': I'd rush to get it all done at the last minute, and then I'd think – "I can't do it!""

Dale Winton
Oh dear: Under Pressure, by any chance?

"I had a goal in life, I always knew what I wanted to do, so I had to work hard towards it. I didn't like studying but obviously I needed to do it. So I sorted myself out, knuckled down, studied hard – and passed my exams."

Gladiator Lightning (Kim)
Borderline Super Swot? Maybe not, but definitely Under Control!

Revision

2 MOTIVATION, PRESSURE AND STRESS

2.1 Motivation: 'why revise'?

Why do you think it's helpful – or necessary – to revise for your exams? The answer to this question will help you answer an even harder one: What will keep you going on days when revision seems too tough, or too boring, to take?

If the hard work of revision is going to seem worth doing, and worth sticking at, you need to:

- **Know what** you want, and
- **Know that** revising will help make it possible.

> "Motivation" is your reason for doing something. It's also that sense of determination and purpose you get when you decide that the result will be worth the effort. Some people are motivated by a promise of rewards. Others simply want the feeling of achievement – of finishing what they started, of proving something, of winning.

What will passing exams mean to you?

Check-up Checklist

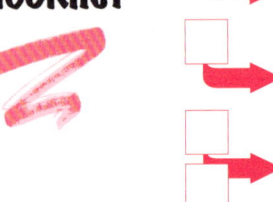

I want to pass my exams because...

☐ I just like to do well at things, particularly [subject/s] _____

☐ I need a pass in [subject/s] _____ to go on to study [subject/s] _____ at [level] _____

☐ I'll need a pass in [subject(s)] _____ to get a job in _____

☐ Qualifications might help when I apply for studies/jobs later on.

☐ My mum/dad wants/expects me to do well.

☐ [Person] _____ has promised me [reward] _____ if I do well.

☐ Other _____

> If you didn't put anything, think what you're saying: you don't care if you pass or not? Really? Well, we can't force you to believe that passing exams does good and feels great! (It does both.) But please talk to someone about this. It's your Number 1 problem!
>
> If your motivation depends on things you want (whether results or rewards), you're on your way: simply use this page to remind you why you're doing it all, when things get tough.
>
> If your motivation is based on things other people want, PAUSE. Do they want the same things for you that you want? Are they expecting too much – or just trying to bring out your best efforts? Do you feel motivated – or pressurised? Talk it over with them, if you can.

What will revising do for you?

Read (revise!) Unit 1.1 and complete the following sentence (like you mean it...)

I KNOW (DEEP DOWN) THAT SENSIBLE REVISION (HOWEVER HORRIBLE IT SEEMS AT THE TIME) CAN MAKE A DIFFERENCE EVEN TO MY EXAM GRADES, BY HELPING ME TO _____

MOTIVATION, PRESSURE AND STRESS

2.2 Understanding stress

What causes stress?

The feelings of quiet desperation that we call stress are often associated with **overwork** and **pressure**: the inability of our body and mind to cope with a particular challenge. But revision and exams are loaded with all sorts of other stress factors. For example:

Boredom	→	Not enough work? (It is possible!) Not enough variety?
Loneliness	→	Not enough time with friends and family? No-one to talk to?
Feelings of guilt	→	Trouble starting? Not enough progress?
Feelings of fear	→	Too many unknowns? Too much left to chance?
Lifestyle	→	Not enough food? Sleep? Exercise? Daylight? Fresh air?

Stress: n. mental, emotional or physical strain or tension.

What does it do to you?

SURPRISING – BUT TRUE: Stress can be good for you! Being 'up against it' boosts your concentration and energy levels – and in fact, most people need some pressure to bring out the best in them!

But uncontrolled stress or too much stress causes STRAIN. And that can be a problem.

Check-up Checklist

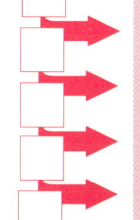

- Irritability, sensitivity and emotional reactions (like bursting into tears)?
- Inability to sleep, or dreaming about revision and exams?
- Inability to concentrate on anything for long?
- Unusual problems with your skin or digestion, headaches and so on?
- Feeling depressed and hopeless about things in general?
- Wanting to avoid other people, when you're normally a sociable type?

If you notice yourself experiencing two or three of these things at once – and they're not normal for you – you may be under strain. It's not pleasant, and it can affect your revision and exam performance if you don't get it under control.

SOS! Signs Of Strain!

SO...

✗ Don't
Try to be laid back, if you're not. Pretend to be laid back, if you're not.

✓ Do
Let your stress work for you. Keep your stress under control.

Danger points

Do you think of yourself as a laid-back person – or do you get stressed quite easily? Write down here any things that seriously wind you up, and that you'll need to deal with.

....
....
....

Where to next?

Super Swot or Under Control? See Unit 2.3

Under Pressure or Getting Desperate? See Unit 2.4

MOTIVATION, PRESSURE AND STRESS

Problems?

Family matters

Things get pretty intense when Tom's revising!

"Everyone is very wary around me. They don't come in without knocking, or speak to me too loudly. Perhaps sometimes I'm outrageous in my demands for silence, and it can cause a bit of friction – because of course they can't all keep quiet all the time. But often it takes a while for me to see that without actually getting annoyed!"

OK, Tom: understanding is clearly required all round! Don't forget, there's always school or the library…

"My sister went to the same school. She's three years older and she was a bit of a swot. That was really hard, because everybody expects you to go along the same lines… but no two people are the same, especially brothers and sisters. One always has to work harder than the other – and I did!"

Kim also told us she got some revision *help* from her sister. Worth a try? Thanks, Kim!

Sometimes people think their parents expect more of them than they actually do. It might be worth finding a suitable moment (*not* in the middle of a row about revising…) and talking with either or both parents, saying: look, what happens if I fail? See how everyone feels. Discuss positive fall-back options. You don't necessarily have to be brilliant at exams to get what you – and your parents – want for your life.

It may help to talk to someone other than your parents, if you feel they're part of the Pressure Problem. Perhaps an older friend, another relative, a favourite teacher – or one of the Revision Helplines on the radio and TV near exam time. But if you feel confused or desperate about revision and exams: talk to *someone*.

MOTIVATION, PRESSURE AND STRESS

Get a life!

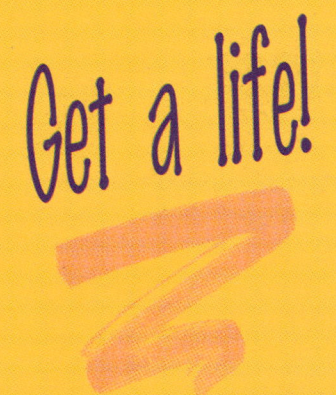

The Amazing Slow Deep Breathing Exercise

Find a quiet place. Sit up straight, hands open in your lap. Close your eyes. Breathe all the way out, until you think your lungs are empty – and then hold for a count of 3. Now let go, let your lungs fill up with air, and let your 'stomach' expand as well as your chest – then hold for a count of 5. Breath out again, slowly, and keep breathing deeply (though not necessarily like that first 'clean-out' breath) for a couple of minutes. Listen to your breathing. If thoughts come into your head, imagine yourself breathing them out – just let them go, and concentrate on breathing again. You'll be amazed how this works!

The Great Bedtime Clench-and-Calm Exercise

Try this when you're lying in bed, trying to get to sleep. Start by clenching your toes, as hard as you can: *hold* for 10 seconds, then relax. Next, stretch the balls of your feet. Next, flex your ankles. Then your calf muscles. Work your way up, a piece at a time, until you've grimaced with your mouth and teeth, and scrunched up your eyes. Just lie there and feel the looseness and heaviness in all your muscles …

STRESS BUSTERS

Fantasy Revision!

Try a Deliberate Daydream, in which you finish your last exam and set off for a major celebration with your friends, or a special holiday. Visualise it: try and be there! If this gets boring (as if!), try another scenario: your exam results arrive, you open them, you can see … whatever grade you want! … Doesn't it feel GREAT?

Do you like…?

Having someone do your hair?
A long hot soak in the bath?
Listening to your favourite music?
Watching a totally silly video?
Playing with your dog or cat?
A completely manic game of football?
… WELL, DO IT! for major stress-free zones …

"When I get nervous… Well, there's nothing quite as helpful as chewing the end of a pencil, is there?"

Birds of a Feather's Pauline Quirk

Revision

13

MOTIVATION, PRESSURE AND STRESS

2.3 Stress – for early starters

The good news is: the earlier you start your revision, the less stressful it's likely to be! But there are still a few things you'll need to watch out for...

Winding up? If you've started your revision campaign early, you're probably a well-motivated and conscientious person. Just check, from time to time, that you're not *so* well-motivated and conscientious that you're turning into a swotaholic! Remember that lack of fresh air and fun can contribute to stress, just as much as worry and time pressure.

action ▶ Check Unit 3.5

Winding down? If you're pacing yourself for the long haul, you may find it difficult to get *enough* stress to stay sharp and bring out your best work! Be sure to build variety into your revision sessions. (Try a few past questions under 'exam conditions' – with time limits. An excellent way of putting a little bit of pressure back into revision!)

action ▶ Check Unit 5.2

2.4 Stress – when time is tight

It's a simple equation. The shorter your revision time and the longer your list of still-to-be-revised topics, the greater the pressure of work and worry.

The obvious solution is to work longer hours: pack in those topics! But look at it this way.

You drive yourself harder → You get more stressed out → You get more tired → You take less in → You have more to do in less time → (cycle repeats)

Prescription for workaholics
- Rest
- Relaxation
- Recreation

Take daily (with food)

Prescription for worriers
- 1 Exam Kit
- Revision (to taste)
- 1 sense of proportion

Take daily (with a pinch of faith)

The healthy solution is to:

- Take time for Revision Planning. Sort out your priorities, and cut out unnecessary work and worry.

action ▶ See Unit 3.4

- Make time for Breaks. Seriously. Suddenly depriving yourself of the sleep, exercise and human contact you're used to may dull the workload-related stress, but ADDS other strains on your system.

action ▶ See Unit 3.5 if you need convincing!

MOTIVATION, PRESSURE AND STRESS

Action Checklist

- ➤ **Start revising as early as possible.** Give yourself time. If it's too late for that, tell yourself that you can still do it – using efficient revision techniques.

- ➤ **Make a revision plan.** Uncertainty and the need to 'improvise' under pressure are a cause of stress for most people. Planning really helps.

- ➤ **Cut down on the unknowns.** Revise as thoroughly as you can. And look at some past exam questions, so you'll know what to expect from the exam.

- ➤ **Take regular (scheduled) breaks.** Your revision will be more pleasant and more effective, in short bursts.

- ➤ **Build in variety.** Monotony, or sameness, is very stressful: if you vary your subjects, revision methods and break-time activities, you'll suffer less.

- ➤ **Be flexible.** If you miss a session, don't load yourself with guilt. Simply plan to catch up later. You're in control of your revision plan – not the other way around!

- ➤ **Be kind to yourself.** Fresh air and physical activity are great confidence boosters, and help you to concentrate – as well as keeping you healthy. Eat and sleep normally and don't rely on coffee or chocolate (or worse!) to keep you going.

- ➤ **Have some fun.** Reward yourself for achieving work goals by doing things you really enjoy in your breaks. This helps to relax you – and keeps exams in proportion.

- ➤ **See your friends.** Isolation is stressful. Use your breaks to be with people – and to find out that you're not alone. Unless you are a really strong person, though, avoid others who are panicking about revision and exams: stress can be 'catching'!

- ➤ **Do your best – not anybody else's.** Don't compare your progress or methods with others' – especially just before or after an exam. Decide what works for you and stick with it. The same goes for results. Don't measure 'success' or 'failure' by others.

- ➤ **Get help where you can.** If you hit a problem, or things get too much for you, don't be a hero: tell someone. A parent or teacher, talked to sensibly, may come through with good advice, or helpful backup – as well as tea and sympathy!

- ➤ **Have a bit of faith.** You almost certainly know – and remember – more than you think. This Exam Kit will give you the added edge of effective revision and exam technique. It is extremely difficult to fail an exam, unless you want to! You've got every chance of doing yourself justice: don't waste it by worrying.

- ➤ **Keep a sense of proportion.** Revision and exams are hard work. But they're over soon, holidays follow – and life goes on! (Turn the page, if in doubt!)

PANIC BUSTERS

Revision

MOTIVATION, PRESSURE AND STRESS

2.5 Keep a sense of proportion

The pressure to do well may come from fear of failure or fear of disappointing other people's expectations. Obviously, you can't stop your parents and teachers from wanting the best for you, and if you have goals which require exam success, you must go for them with all you've got. But try and get things into perspective.

Exam results are important, but not the ultimate decider of your future: at every stage of your life, whatever your grades, you have choices. The worst that can happen is that you have to choose from a different set of options than you'd hoped – and go to Plan B – or choose to retake your exams, to get the results you need for Plan A. OK: you may feel now that you could never go through exams again – but you can and will, if it's important enough to you. You may decide that there are other things you want that don't depend on exam grades...

"I always used to think of myself as the thickest in the class."

Nice one, Bianca!

Richard Branson failed Elementary Maths three times – but things seem to have added up for him since...

Ranulph Fiennes said in a newspaper interview that he only became a world-famous explorer – because he didn't do well in his 'A' levels...

But first of all...
BE POSITIVE ABOUT PASSING – NOT FEARFUL OF FAILURE!

"It's important to think positive when you're going into a pressure situation. For me, playing rugby, I think about the times things have gone well and I go into the game believing it's going to go well... Think about the work you have done, not the work you haven't done: do what you can."

REVISION PLANNING

3.1 Why plan your revision?

Which of the following do you associate with the idea of 'revision planning'?

TIME-WASTING   DEPRESSING   DIFFICULT   INFLEXIBLE   NOT 'ME'
WHAT?   STRESSFUL   BORING   UNNECESSARY

The bad news is: planning is ESSENTIAL, if you are going to do yourself justice in any exam – and especially in more than one. (Yes, we know you've heard this before and it's a real yawn, but take it on board: no plan, no pass...)

The good news is: planning really does make your revision
less stressful – cutting down the uncertainty of making it up as you go
more efficient – saving you wondering-what-to-do-next time
more effective – spreading your time across more topics and subjects.

If it's difficult or depressing – perhaps you're not doing it right!

Quick, simple and flexible?

Basically, a revision plan needs only two elements:

Topics ▶ For a good idea of what you need to cover, look at the headings of your class notes, or the Contents Pages of your textbook or Study Guide.

Time ▶ How many weeks or days have you got before the exams? How many hours do you want to work today? When?

A plan is simply a decision: I WILL DO ...... [TOPIC/S] AT (OR IN) ...... [TIME].

So your revision plan might be a timetable, showing what topics (and breaks) you intend for every half-hour from now to the exams. OR it could simply be a note of two or three topics you want to get done by the end of a day.

Not sure when to start revising? See Unit 1.2

Having trouble sticking to your plan? See Section 4

Make a plan you think you'll be able to stick to.
Be flexible, once you see how things are going. You may fall behind, or even get ahead. So? Add an hour's revision. Add a day off. You're in control.

Start with a plan you *intend* to stick to – and then keep it up-to-date with the real world.

Go for it!

Let's get the spadework over and done with – and make the planning easy!

☐ ▶ For each exam subject, make a list of all the topic areas you think you'll need to revise. (Try the sources suggested above.)

☐ ▶ Find out when your first exam is. Count the number of weeks from now until then, minus one (the week before the exam).

REVISION PLANNING

3.2 Planning for timetable types

Some people are timetable types, and some aren't. Timetable types are quite good at estimating how long a task is going to take them. They try to finish tasks when they are supposed to. If you're not sure this is you, it may *still* be worth giving a timetable a go – just for a week: it is the most effective way of planning revision. (But don't panic: Unit 3.3 offers an alternative approach...)

Action Checklist

Drawing up a timetable

☐ Draw up a blank timetable for all the weeks you have available between now and your first exam. (Or photocopy the one opposite.) Divide each day into hourly or half-hourly sessions from 9 am to 9 pm: don't worry – it won't all be studying!

☐ Enter your *commitments*: times when you will *not* be able to revise. Include:

- lesson (and break) times at school – including 'extras', like sport, and travel time
- meal times (very important!)
- other activities in your normal routine – like household chores.

☐ Now enter '*appointments with yourself*'. Choose and enter:

- One Big Thing per day that is really important to you and **FUN**: meeting friends, your favourite soap, or whatever, plus
- two other things per day that will not take long, but that will make your life easier and more 'normal': a bit of fresh air, a break to listen to music and so on.

Space them out over your day if possible. Don't let them take up too much time: two hours (max) for your One Big Thing, and half-an-hour to an hour for the others.

> If you are starting your revision late, your timetable will need to be a little 'tougher'. See Unit 3.4 for some pointers and warnings, before you start drawing up your plan...

The 'open' times left on your timetable are for revision, and you should enter what you intend to study in each hourly or half-hourly period. Over the page, you'll find some further tips on how to map out which subjects to study, in what order, and for how long.

Go for it!

Take a copy of the timetable opposite and work through our checklist, for the current week.

Enter the things you *regularly* have to do, and will be doing throughout your revision period, in RED ink, so you'll remember to transfer them to each new weekly timetable, when you actually start scheduling revision weeks.

My Timetable

Monday's date: ___/___/19___

	9am–10am	10am–11am	11am–12pm	12pm–1pm	1pm–2pm	2pm–3pm	3pm–4pm	4pm–5pm	5pm–6pm	6pm–7pm	7pm–8pm	8pm–9pm	9pm–10pm	10pm–11pm
Monday														
Tuesday														
Wednesday														
Thursday														
Friday														
Saturday														
Sunday														

REVISION PLANNING

Filling in the blanks

Now you need to decide what topics to revise when. Here are some guidelines.

Action Checklist

☐ → Start with a complete list of all the topics you think you need to revise. (Do the Go for It! Exercise on page 17, if you haven't already!)

☐ → Mark with an asterisk (*) topics that you think you'll need more time on, and those that are important for the exam: your teacher can help you decide.
(These are PRIORITY TOPICS: they have the first claim on your revision time.)

☐ → Match up the number of topics with the number of available revision sessions on your timetable. Ideally, you could cover each topic at least once – but if time is tight and you need to skim or skip topics, your revision priorities get extremely important

Bigger topics may need to be broken down into manageable chunks and spread over a number of sessions so that each session's work target is: • specific and
• realistic.

action — see Unit 3.4.

☐ → Enter each topic into a session (or sessions).

But first, just two more things to consider!

Top tip

If you're starting more than 5 weeks before the exams, leave the last week out of your calculations – and blank on your timetable. If you can't afford a week, leave three days. (See Unit 6.3 for some good reasons why.)

BLOCKS OR BITS?

Will you revise all your science in a block of sessions, then all your maths and so on? Or will you revise a session or two of science, then some maths, a bit of English, some more science and so on?

It's up to you. Some people concentrate better with a 'one track mind', sticking with one subject for a whole day.
Most people, though, prefer to vary subjects within a day: try it yourself.

WHAT WORKS WHEN?

Will you get Priority Topics out of the way early in the day or week, while you're fresh – or do you need some 'ease-in' sessions under your belt first? Get to know your own work patterns: when do you study best?

Check-up Checklist

Are you a **morning** person?
A **late night** person?
Moody just before lunch?
Sleepy just after lunch?
Grumpy on Monday mornings?
Distracted on Friday evenings?

MY BEST STUDY TIMES ARE ✎ _____

_____

MY WORST STUDY TIMES ARE ✎ _____

_____

Where to next?

Less than 4 weeks before the exam?
See Unit 3.4

More than 4 weeks before the exam?
See Unit 3.5

REVISION PLANNING

3.3 Planning for non-planners

It's worth having a go at using a timetable – just once. (See Unit 3.2) But if you know you can't stick to schedules, here's the alternative.

Don't think 'TIME': think 'GOALS'

A timetable tells you to spend an hour revising a topic. The *goal* approach says: never mind the time – finish the topic! A sensible way of planning this way is using a CHECKLIST.

Action Checklist

Start with a Master List of all the topics you think you need to revise, for all subjects.

➤ Put an asterisk (*) against topics that will need more time or are more important: your teacher can help you decide. These are PRIORITY TOPICS.

➤ Divide the number of days available for revision (not counting the last week before the exams: see Unit 6.3) by the number of Priority Topics. The answer is the number of Priority Topics that must go on your Daily Worklist if you're going to cover them all before the exams.

Number of days: ☐   Number of Priority Topics: ☐
Priority topics per day: ☐

➤ Each evening, pick your Priority Topics and add the same number of quicker/easier topics. This is your Daily Worklist for the following day.

➤ Tackle your Daily Worklist in any order, at any time, and check topics off as you feel happy with them. Just keep in mind that – ideally – you want to have ticked off most of the topics on your list for that day: try and pace yourself.

➤ At the end of the day, cross your finished topics off your Master List. If you feel that a Priority Topic could do with another session, simply leave it on, and you'll get to it again later.

➤ If you haven't done all your topics for the day, put the remaining ones at the top of your Daily Worklist for the next day, and add your selection of fresh topics for that day.

➤ If you finish all your topics for the day *early*, it's up to you whether you fit in a few extra topics – perhaps some easier ones. But the time is yours: you've earned it. So make it time off, if you want!

For more advice on prioritising, especially if time is tight: see Unit 3.4.

Unsure what topics to pick? See 'Blocks or bits?' on page 20.

Unsure when to study what? See 'What works when?' on page 20.

Two top tips

- Work in short bursts: a maximum of 50 minutes, with a 10 minute break. We explain why in Unit 3.5.
- Break your topics down into manageable chunks. Set yourself **specific** and **realistic** targets for each revision session.

Go for it!

Copy (or photocopy) the Daily Worklist format overleaf. If you haven't made a Master Topic List, put 'Make Topic List: subject title' (for each subject) on the list.
• Date it today. • Work on through the checklist. • You're on your way!

DAILY WORKLIST

Day and date _____

Brought forward from yesterday's worklist

Priority topics

Subject	Topic	Specifically...	Done? (✔)
			❏ ❏ ❏ ❏ ❏

Filler topics

Subject	Topic	Specifically...	Done? (✔)
			❏ ❏ ❏ ❏ ❏

Today's new topics

Priority topics

Subject	Topic	Specifically...	Done? (✔)
			❏ ❏ ❏ ❏ ❏

Filler topics

Subject	Topic	Specifically...	Done? (✔)
			❏ ❏ ❏ ❏ ❏

SOS! Signs Of Slippage!

If topics are 'carried over' for several days, and your list is getting longer and longer, STOP – and start fresh. This time, try:
- working longer each day, or
- working more quickly and efficiently – or less thoroughly – on each topic, or
- setting yourself fewer topics each day. (Risk of revision gaps: see Unit 3.4.)

REVISION PLANNING

3.4 Extra tips when time is tight

Compare the number of Topics you want to revise with the Time available for revision – as of now! If you end up with more topics per day than you can manage – with breaks, meals and at least seven hours sleep – you'll need to adjust your plan. Here are some options.

Fit in extra revision time

- Make your working day longer. But you need to be very honest and realistic about how many hours you can keep going without blowing a fuse.

- Drop some of your non-revision activities, to free up extra work time. Start with optional ones: think carefully about what is important to you – and to other people. Don't drop the One Big Thing per day that is your real treat.

- Let your revision run into the week before the exams – but *still* not the last two or three days: see Unit 6.3.

> **TOO BUSY NOT TO TAKE A BREAK?**
> Breaks are tough to take when time is tight. But dare to do it. See Unit 3.5.

The more topics you revise, the more questions you'll be equipped to answer, and the more choice and confidence you'll have. BUT, if you haven't got time to do it all...

Tighten your priorities

SKIM or SKIP (in the following order):

- Topics you are already confident you could answer a 'big' question on. (Be honest – and test yourself before you decide.)

- Topics which are unlikely to come up in the exam. (Warning! Very few topics come safely into this category. Check with your teacher.)

- Topics which are difficult for you, and will take up a lot of revision time – but won't earn you many marks (because they only feature on multiple choice papers, say).

- Topics which are difficult for you, and will take up a lot of revision time – but which you feel you'll *still* not be confident enough to answer a 'big' question on.

DON'T SKIM or SKIP topics in syllabus areas where you might get a Compulsory Question.

> **HOW LOW CAN YOU GO?**
> Try to be well prepared on about twice as many topics as there are questions in the exam.
> That way, you'll have a good chance of being ready for the topics the examiner picks!

Priority Topics are:

The most important topics...

- likely to come up in the exam
- may come up as 'big' (high-mark) questions
- may form a compulsory question
- required in order to understand other topics

...where revision will make most difference

- difficult – needing extra help
- 'big' – needing extra time
- complex – needing active revision and practice
- easy – needing just a boost, for real confidence

Top tip

Efficient revision means using less time to gain more confidence. Your 'best bet' topics are those where just a moderate revision effort will equip you to answer exam questions well. When time is tight, keep these topics at the top of your list!

REVISION PLANNING

3.5 How long should a revision session be?

You'll be tempted to try and work for hours without a break. Especially at night. And as the exams approach, you're more likely to feel – or be told – that you're not working hard enough, than that you're not taking enough breaks! But here are the facts.

Short bursts

Make it short! Make it count!

- **You concentrate better in short bursts.** In a two-hour study slot, you'll work faster and better if you:

    study 25 minutes and break for 5 minutes (four times) or
    study 50 minutes and break for 10 minutes (twice)

    than if you study for the full two hours in one go!

- **You take in and remember more in short bursts.** Like your stomach, your brain gets 'full': it needs to digest what you've fed into it, before it can take any more.

> Do you ever find, at a certain point, that you haven't taken in what you've been reading for the last few minutes?
>
> It's called Saturation Point: time to let things settle.

- **You get less tired in short bursts.** You can keep going over a longer working day, if you break up the time. And you're less likely to suffer eye strain, headache, backache, hunger pangs and so on!

Short breaks

Prescription for the real 'three Rs'
- REST
- RECREATION
- RELAXATION

- **Breaks motivate you to get down to work.** Breaks, and what you do with them, are something to look forward to. That session won't seem so bad if you know you'll be due for a break and a treat in a short while.

- **Breaks help you stick to your revision plan.** You need refreshment, fresh air, exercise, other people – and fun – on a regular basis. By allowing for these things in your schedule, you stop them from stopping you getting down to uninterrupted work during your study time.

- **Breaks give you a chance to de-stress.** Switching off is very important, if you're not going to let exams get to you. As long as the break is short and/or scheduled, it shouldn't load you with guilt, either: it's the only way to revise sensibly!

4 GETTING DOWN TO IT, STICKING AT IT

4.1 Why is revising so hard?

Nobody *likes* revising. Really. It's a pain. Getting down to it, and sticking at it – not just through one session, but session after session, day after day – is hard. And the thing is, the more you put it off the worse it seems; and the worse it seems, the more you put it off; and... You get the idea.

But you can break the cycle: first of all, by understanding the problem.

Everybody else has a theory about why you're having trouble getting into your revision. You need to work out what *your* problem is, and if necessary, talk it over with those who give you a hard time.

Why are you putting it off?

> I think I find it hard to get down to revising because:

Does this word ring a bell?

Procrastinate: vb. to put off (an action) until later

Check-up Checklist

☐ I just can't see the point.
action ➤ Motivation: see Unit 2.1 before going on

☐ It's a huge task: I don't know where to start.
action ➤ Planning: see Section 3 before going on

☐ I don't know how to go about it.
action ➤ Work through this Kit: you're on your way!

☐ I can't face it: I feel desperate just thinking about it!
action ➤ Stress: see Units 2.2–2.5 before going on

☐ I don't know, really, something always 'crops up'...
action ➤ Are you sure there isn't another reason behind this? If not, you may actually have a Pure Procrastination Problem! Don't Panic: this section will get even *you* working!

How are you putting it off?

Recognise plan-busters for what they are – and get to know which ones you fall for most!

The following activities are fine – during scheduled free time. If you catch yourself doing them in a timetabled revision slot, or start to feel – deep down – that you're using them to avoid working, note them here.

SOS! Signs Of Slacking

☐ Watching TV (especially programmes you don't really like)
☐ Making tea/coffee/sandwiches – just to keep you going...
☐ Deciding that you/your dog/someone else's dog must get some exercise. Now.
☐ Remembering a friend that you haven't phoned/seen for ages...
☐ Simply *having* to redraw your revision plan.
☐ Getting your brain going by playing a computer game (or two...or three.)
☐ _____
☐ _____

Where to next?

Unit 4.2 Organising for revising

Unit 4.3 Five ways to get you working

GETTING DOWN TO IT, STICKING AT IT

4.2 Organising for revising

Where to revise

It helps you get into the revision habit if you have somewhere regular to work, so try and establish your own special study space if you can. Wherever you work, check that it has the following.

➡ ☐ A proper surface to work on: a table or desk, with enough room on it for your books, notes and equipment. It needs to be the right height, so that you don't get aching shoulders, back or neck at the end of the day.

➡ ☐ Enough light to see by comfortably, without peering. Natural light is best. If you can't be by a window, a desk lamp is better than overhead lighting, which can be dim and cast shadows.

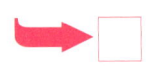

➡ ☐ Privacy, if possible. If you have your own room, use a 'Do Not Disturb' sign, and get it taken seriously! If not, you'll have to negotiate as much peace and quiet as you can get – or find yourself a spot at school or in the local library.

SOS! Suggestions Of Sabotage!

My special study space is
_____
_____

Just say no!

- To telephone calls. Ask someone else to take messages.
- To visits from well-meaning family members, 'just checking you're OK' or offering tea. Encourage this kind of support – but only during your break times.
- To visits from friends, telling you you need to take a break. You will do – but not just then!

Top tip

Get your desk set up for your first study session of the day the night before: otherwise, the preparation will eat into the session itself. Likewise, it's a good idea to tidy up and set up at the end of each study session, ready for the beginning of the next. That way, you'll come back from your break and find yourself ready to go! (Sneaky, huh? No extra excuses...)

Preparation

Get ready to hand all the things you might need for each study session: your revision timetable or checklist, books, Study Guides, class notes, paper, pens, other writing/drawing equipment, and so on.

Keep your desktop tidy: pile books and papers neatly in different areas, so you can find things easily, and have space near you for reading and writing.

Music

Can you *really* work better with background music or TV? Be honest.
And try a few sessions without – or more quietly than usual. You *might* just:
- Concentrate better and remember more
- Enjoy the music/TV more during your breaks, when you can...

TURN IT ON and TURN IT UP!

Problems?

GETTING DOWN TO IT, STICKING AT IT

❝ Too much to do: too little time! And the harder I try to revise, the less I end up doing! ❞

You're expecting too much of yourself. The fear and frustration become a block inside you – until you're unable to face the task. Break it down into small bits – and don't aim at doing too much all at once! Start (today) with just one hour of work. Pick a good time for you. Decide realistically what you can do in that hour, and choose the topic you most feel like doing: one you like, or know a bit about already. The satisfaction of achieving something – however small – will help you move on. Tomorrow, you might do an hour and a half (with breaks!) and perhaps a three hour session at the weekend. Keep your targets realistic – and feel good about yourself: you're on your way and doing fine.

❝ All my friends have got everything done already: I'm way behind. ❞

Ask yourself: why do I think this? Is it because my mates have made a lot of noise about all the work they've done and how marvellous they are? Then again, perhaps they *need* to say that, to boost themselves... Perhaps they're only human, too...

❝ What about the other friends who say 'Come out with us: you're spending too much time working'? I don't want to be really boring... ❞

Again, look at why your friends want you to come out with them instead of working. Are they taking a well-earned break? Do they not need to work? Or have they already given up? Which category are you ready to join them in? Going out may be the right thing to do – at the right time – but it's up to you to decide whether it's worth it. At the end of the day, your exam results are important to you. You don't need to put your friends down, but you have to stand up for yourself to yourself.

GETTING DOWN TO IT, STICKING AT IT

4.3 Ways to get working

So you've listened to 'just one more' record, made 'just one more' cup of coffee – and never quite fitted in that revision session? It's a *real problem*.

First, try to get to the root of the problem and sort that out: see Unit 4.1.

If you still can't seem to get into it? Don't worry: B happy! Here are 5 Bs that will help you make the Breakthrough!

Bully / Kick Start

- Stop and think what you're doing. Imagine passing your exams: how good it will feel – how free you'll be afterwards. Really picture it. Now think what you are risking all this for: unimportant things, which you can do anytime, like after the exams are over – and (specifically) in your scheduled breaks! Smart, huh? Tell yourself not to be so **SAD** (Stupid And Distracted)!

- Start each session with a watch or clock on the table right in front of you, where you can see it all the time. It will loom very large, if you just sit and stare at it – but once you get started, you may even need an alarm clock to tell you when your time is up, you'll be so 'stuck in'!

- Arrange to study with a friend (preferably one who also wants to take revision seriously!). It'll be harder to get out of it, you can spur each other on to keep at it – and you can share a reward at the end of each session.

Brainstorm

'Brainstorming' is simply allowing your brain to throw up ideas, and getting them down on paper – without stopping to organise or criticise them. It's a great way of getting started on topics – and revision sessions!

- Write the topic heading on a sheet of paper – and just start thinking. What do you know about it? What topic areas does it involve? What kind of questions does it raise?

- If nothing occurs immediately, look up your notes on the topic – just to find 3 or 4 key words or phrases (that's not too hard, is it?). Write them on your sheet, and play 'word associations': what comes into your mind when you think of your key words?

- Jot things down as they occur to you – facts, questions, silly ideas and all. When you dry up, stop: you have enough to be going on with. You've got a framework for your revision session – leaving out the silly ideas! And best of all, you've already started!

Try brainstorming your way into essay questions, too! (Hints on how in Unit 9.1.)

GETTING DOWN TO IT, STICKING AT IT

Bribe

- Promise yourself a reward for each session completed or target reached – even if it's only to grab a chocolate bar or phone a friend. Remember, it's a reward : make it **small, specific** and **special** – and available only when you deserve it!

- For longer-term motivation, find a reward that builds up over a day, a week – or the whole revision phase. Give yourself points for sessions completed or targets reached, and devise a range of prizes – from smallish ones (for good daily or weekly points totals) to a mega post-exam prize (for a challenging number of saved-up points).

- Rewards work even better if they are offered by someone else: more chance of their being something you don't normally have – and less chance that you'll cheat! Explain to your family what you're trying to do, and ask for special permissions, financial contributions – or whatever you can come up with.

(More ideas over the page...)

Bluff

If you're really struggling, trick yourself into getting down to work: pretend you're having fun, when actually you're revising. (Instead of the other way round. Just for a change...)

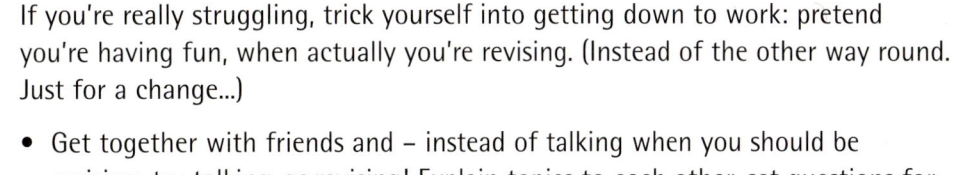

- Get together with friends and – instead of talking when you should be revising, try talking *as* revising! Explain topics to each other, set questions for each other, argue different sides of a question, test each other on facts. We're talking revision!

- Try fitting revision facts and formulas to your favourite songs. When you hear them, sing or rap along. Shock horror: you're revising!

- Stick revision notes in the places you tend to look when you're putting off revising: the phone, the TV, the computer, all your most fabulous posters... Make it a game: if a note catches your eye, you have to read it. Ooops: you're revising again!

If it works for you: do it!
(More ideas in Unit 5.7...)

Believe

- Revision works – when you do. You can get the grades you deserve – or better – if you get down to it and stick at it.

- You can do this. Armed with the Exam Kit, you can revise as well as Super Swot if you have to.

- If you really want to get down to work – right now – *nothing* has to stop you.

Go for it!

You needn't do this now, if you haven't got time – but make it your next revision session!

☐ If you've just been working, take a ten-minute break to do something you really enjoy.

☐ Pick any ONE of our Five B tips, and use it to kickstart one of the following tasks.

☐ If you haven't yet made a Timetable or Worklist, see Unit 3.2 or 3.3 and **do it now!**

☐ If you have made a Timetable or Worklist, identify your next topic and **do it now!**

GETTING DOWN TO IT, STICKING AT IT

Get a life!

STUCK FOR IDEAS ON REWARDS AND CELEBRATIONS? SURELY NOT! Well, we've brainstormed a few to get you in the mood. Add your own wildest ideas, as you think of them. Then offer yourself those rewards – and earn them!

1 Try putting aside money for each session you complete. It needn't be much: if you're working steadily, it adds up to a nice little celebration fund for when it's all over! (You might even talk a parent into doubling your money, if you've really worked hard...)

2 Chocolate: possibly the Number 1 reward choice. Don't eat it if you don't earn it!

3 What's your favourite band? Make up your mind that you'll only listen to that album after a successful revision session. No notes – no notes...

4 Together with friends (in non-revising time, naturally), build up the promise of a day – or evening – out. Start from scratch, and for each full day of revision you put in, add one step or new idea, until you have a complete plan – and a really special occasion!

Revision
30

TOOLS, TACTICS AND TRICKS

5.1 Tools

What are you going to use to help you revise? This is a chance to prepare your revision sessions and to think about what tools you'll need in the exam: make sure you have them – and know how to use them! You may like to photocopy and use the following checklist for each subject.

SUBJECT: _____   **TOPIC:** _____   **DATE:** _____

Source material
- ❏ Class notes and handouts
- ❏ Coursework folder
- ❏ Textbooks
- ❏ Study Guides
- ❏ Exam Kit
- ❏ Dictionary: English/Other
- ❏ Past exam papers/question books
- ❏ Other (List): _____

In advance:
Check: Complete? Correct? Clear?

To borrow from Library? If so, when?

Note-making material
- ❏ Paper: plain/graph
- ❏ Index cards/note pad/Postit notes
- ❏ Pens and pencils: black/blue/coloured
- ❏ Pencil sharpener
- ❏ Eraser/Tippex

Equipment
- ❏ Ruler/set square/compass/protractor
- ❏ Calculator
- ❏ Other (List): _____

Check what the examiner advises.

Check what the exam requires.
Check if allowed in the exam.

People (Sorry, but you can 'use' them too!)
- ❏ Family. I need (List): _____

OK about study space/time/privacy?
Possible source of help?

- ❏ Friends. I need (List): _____

Warned against distraction?
Available/willing to study together?
Got notes/handouts you missed?

- ❏ Teachers. I need (List): _____

Available for advice/help?

- ❏ Other. (List): _____

TOOLS, TACTICS AND TRICKS

5.2 Tactics: passive or active?

Reading is a necessary part of revision, but won't get you very far by itself – even if you have time to read the same material over and over again. Let's face it: simple repetitive reading is BORING! It won't maintain your concentration and you won't really know how much you've taken in.

If you can read *actively* you'll:
- keep your mind and memory stimulated
- keep track of your progress, and
- keep yourself going with the sense that you're *getting* somewhere.

ACTIVE LEARNING simply means doing something – anything – with what you read.

- ☐ Make notes of key points – or questions to follow up later. *check – how do you make notes?*
- ☐ Look up any terms you don't understand, or make a note to do so.
- ☐ Underline or **highlight** points of interest or useful quotations.
- ☐ Pick out key words and topic 'patterns', and write them onto revision slips or cards.
- ☐ Try to make a diagram, flowchart or word game from a list of points.
- ☐ Put aside or cover up your book/notes and test your recall.
- ☐ Try and guess what questions an examiner might ask on a topic – and answer them.
- ☐ Involve other people in discussing or testing you on topics.
- ☐ Have a go at past exam questions.
- ☐ Find teachers' comments on your coursework assignments, and put right anything you got wrong or left out.

ACTIVE NOTE DIAGRAM KEYWORD TEST DISCUSS QUESTION

```
Keyword    Diagram
    \      /
     NOTE
      |
    ACTIVE
      |
     TEST
    /      \
Discuss    Question
```

Compare/contrast active/passive
Define 'active learning'
Benefits of 'active learning'

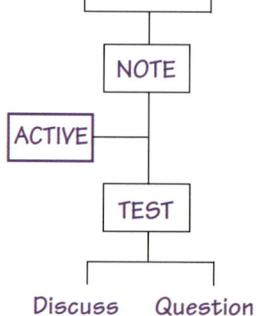

Revise, improvise or memorise?

Exams are not just a test of your memory. Often, you are given data in an exam question, and asked to do something with it. You are being asked to apply what you know, what you've understood: not to reel off facts. However:

- **Foreign vocabulary** may have to be learned by heart – though ideally, in context.
- **Quotations from set literature** can be useful – but resolve to use them only if they're relevant to the exam question!
- **Rules, laws and formulas**, once memorised, can help you to use data correctly. (They mainly apply to grammar and spelling, science and maths.)

Otherwise, go for tactics that increase your understanding – not just your recall!

TOOLS, TACTICS AND TRICKS

5.3 Tactic 1: revision notes

It's only when you look back at your class notes that you can see (a) what's important and (b) the overall 'shape' of the topic. Revision is an ideal opportunity to reduce and rework your notes so that they:

- include only the key points – and are therefore shorter, and
- reflect the relationship between points – and are therefore more memorable.

Lists

A list of key words or phrases is the simplest way to reduce a number of related points.

- Causes of an event
- Characteristics of a thing, place, time
- Traits of a character.

It's a good idea to number the points in your list: it'll jog your memory if you know how many points you're after!

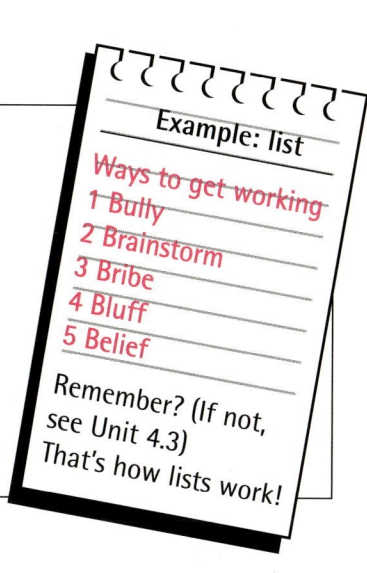

Example: list

Ways to get working
1 Bully
2 Brainstorm
3 Bribe
4 Bluff
5 Belief

Remember? (If not, see Unit 4.3) That's how lists work!

Split lists

Split lists are simply lists of related key points which balance each other.

- Sides of an argument ('for', 'against')
- Alternative solutions to a problem ('either', 'or')
- Advantages and disadvantages
- Similarities and differences ('compare and contrast')

Split lists visually reflect the nature of the relationship between the points, so they're particularly memorable.

Example: split list

Characteristics of Arteries and Veins

ARTERY	VEIN
TUBULAR	
ENDOTHELIUM PRESENT	
TRANSPORTS BLOOD	
THICK WALL	THIN WALL
NO VALVES	POCKET VALVES
CAN CONSTRICT	CAN'T CONSTRICT
BLOOD FROM HEART	BLOOD TO HEART
HIGH PRESSURE	LOW PRESSURE

TOOLS, TACTICS AND TRICKS

Chains

Chains are lists of key points which link in a particular order or sequence: for example, chronological order ('X, then Y, then Z') or cause and effect ('X causes Y, which causes Z').

- Events leading up to a war (or whatever)
- The plot of a novel
- Stages in a process

Your notes could follow a simple line, or a flowchart.

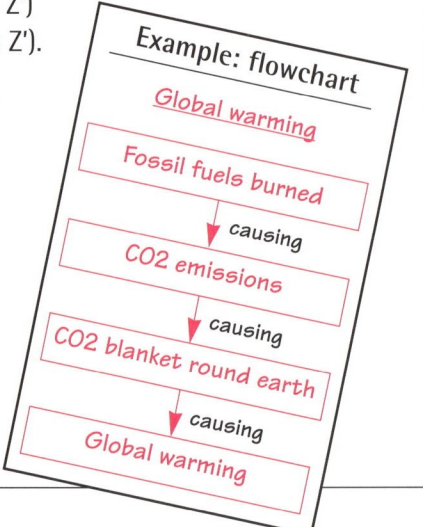

Example: flowchart

Global warming

Fossil fuels burned
↓ causing
CO_2 emissions
↓ causing
CO_2 blanket round earth
↓ causing
Global warming

Go for it!

➡ What underlying 'patterns' can you identify in the following topics? (Suggested answers below...)
  (a) The French Revolution: was it a Good Thing?
  (b) What are the features of a rainforest habitat?
  (c) How do you test whether a substance contains starch?
  (d) What is the length of the third side of a (given) right-angle triangle?

➡ Take a ten minute break!

➡ Pick a fact-type topic from your revision plan. Find your notes on it. Read them.

➡ As you read, note down or highlight any key words or phrases.

➡ Think of a likely question on the topic. (Cause? Compare and contrast? Your opinion?)

➡ Identify its underlying pattern.

➡ On a new sheet, write out your key words or phrases so they reflect that pattern.

➡ Date the sheet – and take a break! You've done some serious revision!

Top tip

Ideally, your final notes on a topic will be brief enough to fit on an index card. Try it. You end up with a pocket (or box) full of Quick Revision Prompters! They don't take up space, they don't take up time – and they are just ace for testing and prompting your recall!
- Note it • Date it • Stack it • Scan it • Test it!
Get the habit...

ESSENTIALS ONLY!

You can make more detailed and complex notes by adding related sub-points and examples:

- as notes below or beside the points on your list (which therefore act as *headings*) or
- linked by extra 'branches' on your chain or flowchart. (For really adventurous versions, see Unit 5.6.)

But remember, your aim is to REDUCE your notes. As you select what's important in a topic, you'll be fixing it in your mind: your key points will be enough to bring it all back to you.

Go For It! Suggested answers: (a) Split list (two points of view) (b) List (c) Chain (sequence of actions in experiment) (d) Ideally, just a mathematical formula!

5.4 Tactic 2: test yourself

Self-testing helps you assess your progress. It is also a highly effective way of revising. There are lots of ways of testing your understanding and recall of what you've revised: try some, mixed into your revision sessions.

Self-Test Techniques

- Put aside or cover up your books/notes and try to jot down the essential points from memory. Check them against the source, for completeness and accuracy.
- Pick one of your brief revision notes or index cards, and expand on it (talking or in writing).
- Get a friend or family member to ask you questions from your notes.
- Explain the topic to someone else – or to yourself in the mirror, or to a favourite poster!
- Debate two-sided questions with a clued-up friend.
- Role-play people and situations from your history, geography or literature.
- Make a list of questions that might be asked about a topic – and give an outline answer, verbally or in writing.
- Analyse and attempt actual past exam questions.

Note any areas you got wrong or didn't feel confident about, and refresh your memory – or plan to do so later! (Seriously. Put it straight on your Master List or Daily Worklist, before you forget!)

Go for it!

- ☐ If you've just been working, take a ten minute break!
- ☐ Pick a topic you've already revised – or revise one now! (See Unit 5.2 if you need to.)
- ☐ Pick one of our Self-Test techniques.
- ☐ If it involves someone else: talk to him or her about it and fix a time to get together.
- ☐ If it's just you: what are you waiting for?

Learning to be flexible: past exam questions

Yes, we know: practising past exam questions sounds boring and a waste of fact-learning time. Of course it is important to know the content of your notes – but few exam questions will allow you simply to reproduce them in their original form and order. In fact, questions are designed to make you:

- select relevant points – those that relate specifically to the question;
- combine relevant points – from different aspects of a topic, or different topics; and
- interpret data – to show you understand the points being raised.

Unless you are flexible in revising, you'll find it hard to be flexible when it comes to applying what you've learned. Past questions help you think about the content of your notes in different ways: explaining, describing, comparing, contrasting and so on.

Past questions also tell you two very important things about the exam.

- How many questions you have to answer, how many marks are available for each, and therefore how long you should take to answer each one. (Useful, huh? Do you want to have to do those sums for the first time in the exam?)
- What types of questions are regularly set. Structured, short answer, essay, multiple choice: they all require something different from you – and you'll lose marks if you don't approach the question properly.

TOOLS, TACTICS AND TRICKS

The good news is that using past questions doesn't have to be a long-winded process.

Here's a Checklist to get you started. Photocopy it, and keep one alongside every question you look at.

Action Checklist

- ☐ How many marks are available for the question? ....
- ☐ How much time should you spend on the question? ....
  [Hint: proportion of total marks = proportion of total time. See Unit 9.2.]
- ☐ What method and length of answer is required? ....
- ☐ What equipment and sources are you allowed/required to use? ....
- ☐ What data, formulae etc. are given to help you? ....

Multiple choice, part-answer and short-answer questions

- ☐ Try them. (They can even be fun!)
- ☐ Check your answers against the Suggested Answers (if any) or your own notes – or ask a teacher.

Essay questions

Depending how much time you want to spend, you might try any of the following. Refer to your revision notes at first, if you need to – but try without, as soon as you feel you can.

- ☐ Practise analysing questions. Read carefully and circle or underline words which:
  - Show what the examiner wants you to do *action* — See Unit 8.2. in your answer.
  - Indicate what topic(s) or topic area(s) the examiner is referring to.
  - Might link with your revision notes and boost your memory.

- ☐ Select a question you feel fairly confident about, and make a brief answer plan: just a list of what your main points and examples would be. Jot down points as they occur to you, at first: then put them in order, under appropriate headings and subheadings. *action* — See Unit 9.1.

  It took me .... minutes to make an answer plan – with/without using my notes.

- ☐ Select a question and actually have a go! This is harder work – but well worth it, especially if you time yourself: it can be a bit of a shock, the first time!

  An answer .... pages long took me .... minutes to write – with/without notes.

- ☐ Check your answers against the Suggested Answers (if any), or your own notes, or ask a teacher. If you've got your facts straight, well done – but make sure you've answered the question!

Go for it!

Take the first step to get hold of some past questions – now. You might start by looking in a Study Guide or Question and Answer book; check the school library; or ask your teacher.

TOOLS, TACTICS AND TRICKS

5.5 Tricks with words

Memory is like putting something in storage: if you attach an identifying 'tag' or 'marker' to it, you'll be able to locate it more easily later on.

'Mnemonic': n. Something to assist memory.

Here are some verbal mnemonic methods – using words and word patterns – to try.

- Use the **initial letters** of the words in lists to make up more catchy phrases or words. This helps you remember all the words in the list, and even their order.

    Colours of the spectrum (in order):
    Red Orange Yellow Green Blue Indigo Violet
    *Mnemonic: **R**ichard **O**f **Y**ork **G**ave **B**attle **I**n **V**ain*

    You could do this for any sequence of letters: the elements in the Periodic Table, say – or a sequence of musical notes.

- Use **word associations** or **puns** to make unfamiliar or technical terms more familiar, or to reinforce the meaning of what you're trying to remember.

    Stalactite? Stalagmite?
    Mnemonic: Tights go down, mites grow up.

- Use **rhymes**:

    Winds do blow from high to low (pressure zones)

- To remember dates, make up a catchy phrase which relates to the event, out of words with the **number of letters** corresponding to the numbers in the date.

    1492 Columbus discovers America
    Mnemonic: A (1) Yank (4) discovery (9), eh (2)?

Your own mnemonics work best – but for extra inspiration, see the Toolbox page overleaf!

Top tip
If a striking mental image is conjured up, even better. Try picturing it in your mind for a few seconds: you'll find it sticks – especially if it's silly (or rude!) This works well for foreign vocabulary, too. If you want to remember that the French for cupboard is 'armoir', try visualising a yokel waving his arm and shouting 'ooh arr!' as he runs into a cupboard!

Go for it!

Devise your own mnemonics for the following.

- ☐ The First World War: 1914–1918
- ☐ The heart takes Oxygenated blood on the Left and Deoxygenated blood on the Right.
- ☐ The order of the first six pilgrims in The Canterbury Tales: Knight, Squire, Yeoman, Prioress, Monk, Friar.

Toolbox

It's best if you make up your own mnemonics – so the following are mainly for ideas and inspirations. But if they work for you, be our guest: take what you need!

Characteristics of living organisms:
Reproduction, Excretion, Movement, Irritability, Nutrition, DEvelopment, Respiration
= REMINDER

The Tropic of Capricorn is the one <u>below</u> the Equator: You have Capri-corns on your feet!

Protons are **P**ositively charged, **N**eutrons are **N**egatively charged.

Trigonometry:

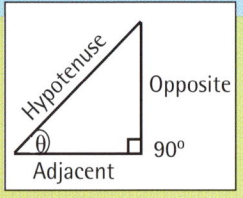

$\sin \theta = \dfrac{\text{Opposite}}{\text{Hypotenuse}}$ $\cos \theta = \dfrac{\text{Adjacent}}{\text{Hypotenuse}}$ $\tan \theta = \dfrac{\text{Opposite}}{\text{Adjacent}}$

Some Old Hippies Cough And Hiccough To Others' Annoyance

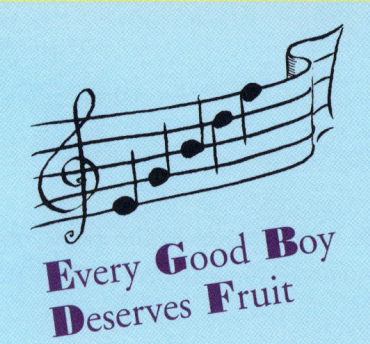

Every **G**ood **B**oy **D**eserves **F**ruit

Causes of Acid Rain:
Emission – Oxidation – Solution – Precipitation
Ecology Offers Some Protection

Battle of Waterloo	French Revolution	Abolition of Slavery
1815	1789	1833
I remember a fight	A royally headless frenchman	A manacled man – not!

Concave or convex? Con-Caves are hollowed out mountains.

Spelling
'I' before 'E', except after 'C', when the sound is 'EE'

Acid reactions
CARBONATE + ACID -> SALT + CARBON DIOXIDE + WATER
ACID rain falls on the CAR BONNET. Dad'll do a somerSAULT if there's WATER on the CD!

Practise or Practice? Advise or Advice?
'-ise' if it's used as a verb – like 'is'!
'-ice' if it's used as a noun – like 'ice'!

Factors in the business environment
Political **E**conomic **S**ocial **T**echnological
They can be a PEST.

French vocab
'Plafond' – 'planchet'. Which is floor, which is ceiling?
Floors have 'planks'

TOOLS, TACTICS AND TRICKS

5.6 Tricks with pictures

Go for it!

Draw a diagram showing how water evaporates from the oceans, condenses in clouds and falls as rain: the water cycle.

It's best if you make your own patterns as you think through a topic. Simply pick out the key words and illustrate or link them visually in any way that seems sensible to you. In Unit 5.3, we showed two visual devices: a split list and a flowchart. Here are two more.

Diagrams

Diagrams are 'pictures' which are reduced to very basic elements, shapes and lines. They are useful for showing component parts – of a flower, say, or a machine. With lines and arrows, you can show systems and processes, too. For example, here's what happens to blood in the circulatory system.

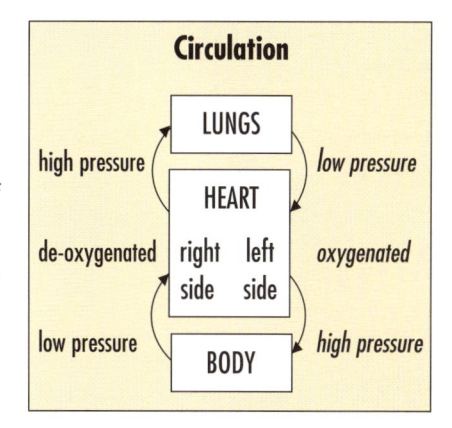

Circulation

```
              LUNGS
high pressure ↗   ↘ low pressure
              HEART
de-oxygenated right | left oxygenated
              side  | side
low pressure ↘   ↗ high pressure
              BODY
```

Mind maps

'Mind maps' sound complicated, but needn't be. They are amazingly effective as a way of analysing and remembering topics – definitely worth a go! Here's how. Start with your main topic or theme title in the middle of a page, in a box. Add the main areas or points within the topic/theme, linked to the central box by lines or 'branches'. As points divide further, or lead on to others, branch out again.

Branches link points that are logically connected: add labels if you want to note what the connection is – 'eg' [for example], 'leads to' or whatever you choose. Keep it tidy: use key words and phrases (or symbols or pictures) only. Use capital letters, boxes, circles, colour, underlining or whatever it takes to make more important elements stand out – and to make the whole thing memorable!

Top tip

Mind map as you brainstorm ideas or work through notes: add branches as things occur to you – and don't worry if they're all over the place! Later, redraw your map more neatly.

Go for it!

Pick a topic and try one: it's fun! If you'd like a bit of extra help, check out the formats in the Toolbox pages overleaf...

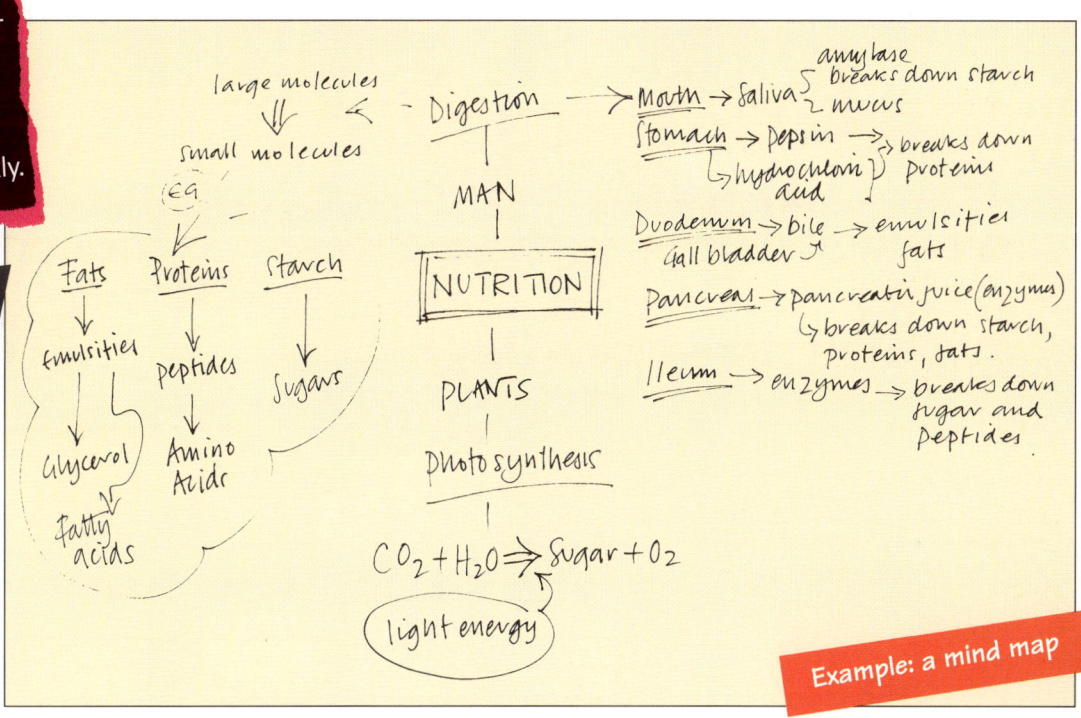

Example: a mind map

Toolbox

Try some of the following formats. We've left them blank, so you can copy them and put in your own data.

Compare and contrast

Features of _____

Common features →

Features of _____

Process/method

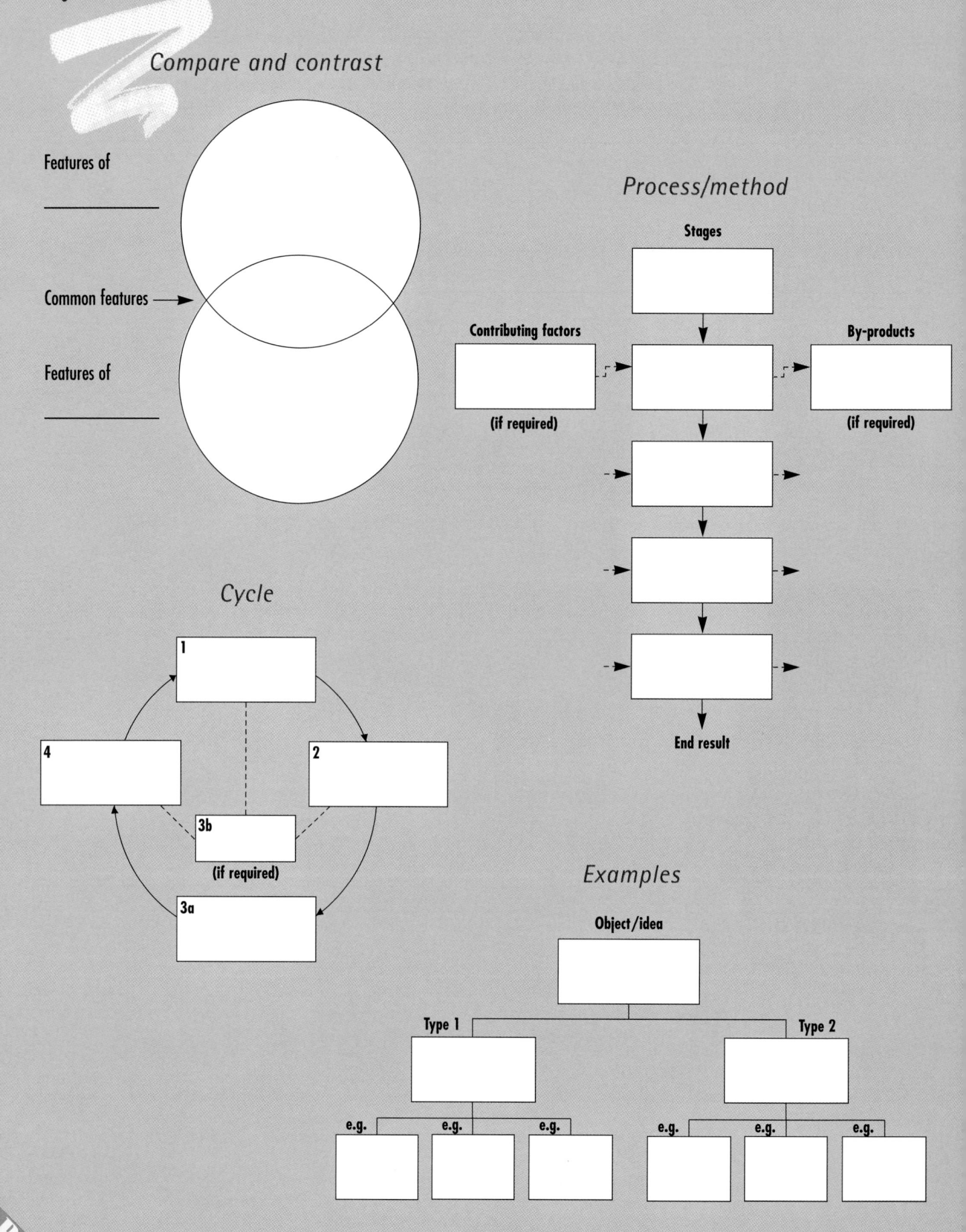

Stages

Contributing factors (if required)

By-products (if required)

End result

Cycle

1
2
3a
3b (if required)
4

Examples

Object/idea

Type 1 — e.g., e.g., e.g.

Type 2 — e.g., e.g., e.g.

Toolbox

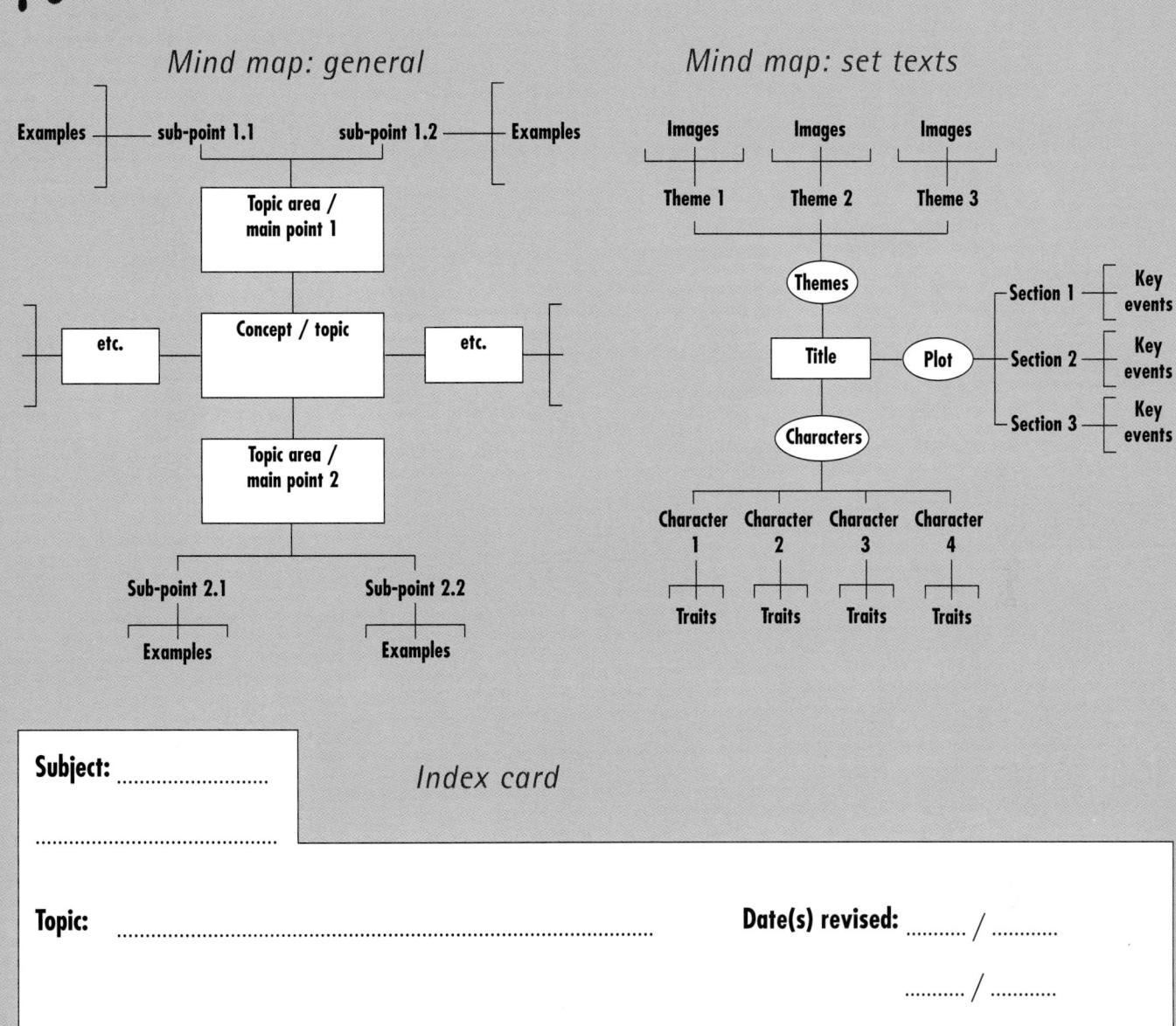

TOOLS, TACTICS AND TRICKS

Mind map: general

Examples — sub-point 1.1   sub-point 1.2 — Examples

Topic area / main point 1

etc. — Concept / topic — etc.

Topic area / main point 2

Sub-point 2.1   Sub-point 2.2

Examples   Examples

Mind map: set texts

Images   Images   Images

Theme 1   Theme 2   Theme 3

Themes

Title — Plot — Section 1 — Key events
              — Section 2 — Key events
              — Section 3 — Key events

Characters

Character 1   Character 2   Character 3   Character 4

Traits   Traits   Traits   Traits

Index card

Subject: ....

....

Topic: ....

Date(s) revised: .... / ....

.... / ....

.... / ....

Revision

TOOLS, TACTICS AND TRICKS

5.7 Whatever works

Get a life!

If you have a problem, get round it. If you have an interest, use it. Revision doesn't have to be grim. So don't be SAD (Swotty And Desperate)!

Role-play characters and situations from history or literature, with your friends. Put baddies on 'trial'. Have a debate, saying why each person deserves to live. Play rival detectives in a 'whodunnit' (and why) to unravel events. Whatever!

Use music... or not. If you think music helps you revise, play it quietly in the background. If it distracts you, turn the radio/stereo off and use music as a reward. Turn it up when you take a break. Reward yourself with your favourite track when you've completed a certain length of revising.

Stick keyword notes in 'thought bubbles' on your favourite posters.

R-r-r-r-r-r-revision! Rap it!

Charlotte likes to use a highlighter pen. It can be that simple.

Chris likes to use bullet points in his notes, to pick out important things.
- "There's probably just as much information," he told us.
- "But it looks like less... So it doesn't put me off so much!"

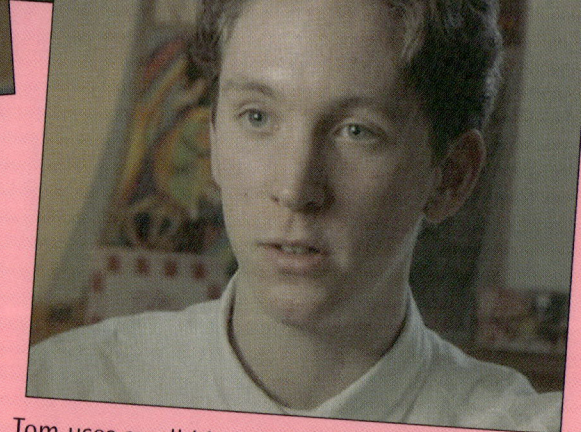

Tom uses small bits of paper for his notes, so he really has to reduce them - if they're going to fit!

Noreen's handwritten notes are enough to scare her off revision altogether! But once she's got them condensed, she types them up into a neat layout that doesn't look too crowded. They're easier to revise from - and they've been through one more active process!
Noreen also told us she sticks key-point notes on her door, so she can't help 'revising' whenever she goes out! Cool idea...

TOWARDS THE EXAM

6.1 Winding up?

The final run-up to exams can be a particularly nerve-wracking time – for two main reasons.

> I'm actually going to have to take an exam!

It will help if you:

- Use your remaining revision time to cut down on the unknowns. Look at past papers: get to know how many questions you'll have to attempt, what sort they are, how long you've got, what you're allowed to take in with you – and so on.
  action ▶ See page 45.

- Get into some stress management techniques (if you haven't already...)
  action ▶ See page 13.

Think of it this way: the hard slog is coming to an end! Hang in there and it'll soon be *PARTY TIME!*

> So much to do, so little time!

The exams are no worse than before – only closer!
If you think you've got too much to do in the time:

Don't panic: **prioritise!** Focus on the revision topics that will give you more choices and more chances in the exam.
action ▶ Unit 3.4.

Don't work through breaks, over nights or up to the last minute! At this point, you are **too busy <u>not</u> to take a break!** The harder you've worked on your revision, the less you want to blow it by burning out in the last few days before the exam!
action ▶ Units 6.3, 6.4

PANIC BUSTERS

Top tip
If you're too jumpy to sleep, try:
- A hot milky drink before going to bed
- Breathing, clench-and-calm or visualisation exercises (see page 13)
- Reading in bed – something fun and easy
- Keeping a pad by your bed: if you suddenly think of something you have to do, write it down immediately. Then forget it until tomorrow!

6.2 Winding down?

SOS! Smug or Sinking?

If you feel you couldn't care less at this point, it's either:

- Complete confidence (Yes, Super Swot: you know who you are!) or
- Tiredness and fed-upped-ness!

If it's the first, just think: do you want to blow it? Try some strictly timed exam questions, to remind you that you need to stay on your toes!

If you know deep down that it's the second, treat as for 'Winding UP': Unit 6.1 above.

6.3 The week before

If you've followed our advice so far, you won't have any new topics scheduled for the last week before the exam. Use this week to:

- Go back and refresh your memory of essential or difficult points, to boost your confidence
- Catch up, if you've fallen behind your schedule (though you should *still* not try to cover new ground in the last two days)
- Refresh yourself, before the exam.

The temptation will be to keep revising right up to your first exam – and between exams if possible – but you should really allow at least one full day before any exam, in which you do nothing more than look over your briefest and most familiar revision notes and mnemonics.

SOS! Swotting or Swamping?

We're serious about this. There's no point working really hard – and then blowing it by going into the exam exhausted, fed up and burnt out! It can happen!

If you work up to the last minute, you may have covered a few extra topics – but if you're tired you'll find it harder to make connections and to relate the points to the questions in the exam. Take the time out: with a fresh brain, you may even find you remember those final topics better anyway!

Do something relaxing, something you enjoy, something 'normal' for you. And get some fresh air and exercise if possible.

6.4 The night before

It is vital not to tire (or overstuff!) your brain the night before the exam. If you must work, don't work late, and try to get a good night's sleep (see Unit 6.1). Trust us: you won't do as well if you're short of sleep, however many topics you might have crammed in!

If you can't stop thinking about the exam, there are still things you can usefully do: consult your Clear the Decks Checklist. If you really 'must' revise (not that we approve…), only use your briefest notes and mnemonics: if you find a whole new unfamiliar topic, you *know* you'll panic!

Top tip

Don't, at this stage, compare notes with fellow students about how your revision has gone. At least one of you will come out stressed and depressed from the discussion!

Brain food?

There are people who say you must have a hearty breakfast before an exam – but the best advice is to do whatever is most normal for your body and routine. The same with chocolate: don't expect an Instant Brain Boost! The fact is, a sugar 'high' is followed by a *dip* in energy and concentration levels. Stick to what you're used to…

CLEAR THE DECKS!

Action Checklist

SUBJECT: _____   PAPER: _____

The week before

☐ *I know when the exam is*

　Day: _____   Date: _____

　Start time: _____   Finish time: _____

☐ I know where the exam is

　Address of exam centre: _____

　I'll be going there from: _____

　How to get there: _____

　Estimated journey time: _____   Time to set out: _____

☐ *I know a bit about the exam*

　I will have to answer _____ questions, of which _____ may be compulsory.
　I expect ____ Multiple choice, ____ Short answer, ____ Essay-type, ____ Practical, ____ Oral questions.

☐ I know what I need (and am allowed) to take into the exam with me

　For writing/drawing: **Pens (+ colours?), pencils (+ colours?), ruler**

　Special equipment (eg. calculator) : _____

　Books: _____

　Personal (eg medications): **Tissues,** _____ Hayfever?

　Spares & repairs: **eraser, Tippex, pencil sharpener, spare pens,** _____

　Plastic bag to carry all the above.

☐ *I have put away all my class notes and textbooks. My briefest revision notes and mnemonics are all I'm going to look at from now on.*

The night before

☐ I have all the above information.

☐ I have packed everything I'll need for the exam.

☐ I have set my alarm clock for: ....

☐ I HAVE DONE EVERYTHING I CAN. ALMOST THERE...

Exams

So. You've been getting to grips with your course material. Now's the time to find out if you know what to do with it – BEFORE you get into the exam room!

1. Which of the following are you NOT sure about? (More than one, if appropriate.)

A The date/time/location of each exam you'll be taking.
B The equipment you are allowed/advised to take into each exam with you.
C What question types you are likely to get in each exam.
D What question topics are likely to come up in each exam.

2. Which of the following exam-type questions is the 'odd one out'?

A 'Compare x and y'
B 'What is the difference between x and y?'
C 'Distinguish between x and y'
D 'Contrast x and y'

3. Which question on an exam paper (given a choice) will you attempt first?

A The one that looks hardest.
B The first one you see that looks easy.
C The one that looks easiest.
D The one with the most marks available.

4 You've done 4 essays out of 5 – and you have 10 minutes left. What should you do?

A Panic.
B Go back and check and polish the other four answers, for extra marks.
C Do an answer plan, introduction and conclusion to the fifth answer.
D Start the fifth answer and see how far you get.

5. Which of these statements do you think is true? (More than one, if you like.)

A Examiners try to catch you out with trick questions.
B It doesn't matter how tidy your answers look, as long as you get them right.
C If you're really desperate, it's worth trying to smuggle some notes in with you.
D It helps you unwind if you discuss the exam with other people afterwards.

6. What do you think is the most important thing about an exam answer?

A You've shown how much you know about the topic.
B Your spelling, grammar and punctuation are good.
C You've got the right answer.
D You've shown that you've thought about the question set.

7. Which of the following (if any) are you worried about?

A Your mind going blank in the middle of the exam.
B Not seeing a single question you can answer.
C Not understanding the questions.
D Falling behind and not finishing all the questions.

Your score

OK. So what unknowns and niggles do you have? Let's get them sorted.

	Where to? Try Unit(s)...
1. Being prepared	
A, B or C: Shame on you! Check NOW.	Page 45
D: Good for you! You can *never* be sure of the topics that will come up...	
2. Reading questions	
A: Right! Remember to think as carefully in the exam...	
B, C or D: Nope. Check that you know why – and how to read exam questions.	8.2
3. Choosing questions	
A, B or D: You're making life difficult for yourself. Think more clearly about this.	8.3
C: You're on your way to getting some good marks under your belt. Carry on...	
4. Timing answers	
A: You've hit on the one solution that *won't* gain you any extra marks...	7.2
B: or D: Not ideal. Think again and see if you can see why...	9.2
C: You'd have done the best you could to retrieve the situation. Good choice.	
5. Misunderstandings	
A: You're wrong – fortunately! Take it from the examiners...	Page 60
B: You're not entirely wrong: it's good to get the answer right! BUT...	9.3
C: You've picked the second most likely reason for failing an exam! Sort out why...	7.2
D: You won't be doing yourself – or your friends – any favours!	10.1
6. What examiners want	
A: You need to think more about the question...	8.2
B or C: You're right, up to a point: you get marks for those things. BUT...	9.5, 8.2
D: You're well on your way to earning the marks you deserve!	
7. Any other worries?	
A: Don't worry. It rarely happens – and if it does, you can deal with it.	9.6
B: Focus on reading and choosing the questions intelligently. It helps...	8.2, 8.3
C: Focus on topic and instruction key words: they're all you need.	8.2
D: Plan, practise - and have sensible fall-back plans, just in case.	9.2

Contents

7 In the exam room
7.1 Being prepared
7.2 Staying calm

8 The exam paper
8.1 Rubrics, instructions, advice
8.2 Questions, questions!
8.3 Choosing questions

9 Answers
9.1 Planning answers
9.2 Timing answers
9.3 Presenting answers
9.4 Answer tips for question types
9.5 Checking answers
Meet the examiner
9.6 In case of emergency

10 So there is life...
10.1 After the exam
10.2 Between exams
10.3 CONGRATULATIONS!

7 IN THE EXAM ROOM...

7.1 Being prepared

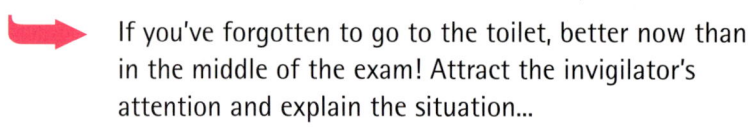

OK. You're there, now. And you're as ready as you can be. Almost...

Pre-flight checks

→ If you've forgotten to go to the toilet, better now than in the middle of the exam! Attract the invigilator's attention and explain the situation...

→ If the exam paper is face up, check that you have the right one – and that you've been given anything else specified on the front cover: answer sheets/booklets and so on. (If the paper is face down, don't turn it over until you're told to.)

→ Check that you have all the writing/drawing equipment you need. If your pen is out of ink – or whatever – now's the time to notice, and ask the invigilator for help.

→ Listen carefully to the invigilator's instructions about how and when to do things.

READY?

7.2 Staying calm

Facing that exam paper at long last, your nerves can threaten to get the better of you. There's no cure, but the following may help!

→ Everyone else feels the same.
Remember: nervousness need not harm your performance – and can actually boost it!

→ Don't think (or talk to others) about how much you know or don't know.
Don't speculate about what might be in the paper.
Try the Deep Slow Breathing exercise (page 13).

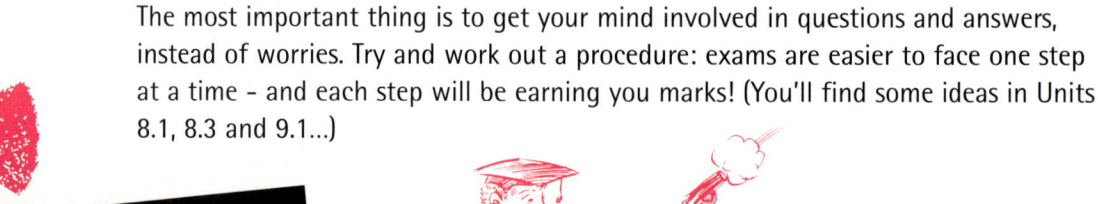

The most important thing is to get your mind involved in questions and answers, instead of worries. Try and work out a procedure: exams are easier to face one step at a time - and each step will be earning you marks! (You'll find some ideas in Units 8.1, 8.3 and 9.1...)

STEADY?

Warning!
Tempted to cheat? Don't even think about it. You won't be trying anything the invigilators haven't seen a thousand times. Besides, cheating doesn't work. *In fact, it's your second-best chance of FAILING the exam. (The best is not to turn up!)* You'll be caught and disqualified. Or you'll be so distracted and stressed that you'll blow it anyway. Just trust your brain...

THE EXAM PAPER

8.1 Rubrics, instructions & advice

> Rubric: n. A set of rules for conduct or procedure.

If you've worked through the Exam Kit, you'll know how much useful information there is on an exam paper – before you even get to the questions! Rubrics, instructions and advice are designed to HELP YOU:

➡ To know – and do – what the examiner wants: the only way to get marks.
➡ To make best use of the time available, to get more marks.
➡ To get started – and get past your nerves.

Action checklist

Kick start

- ☐ Read the Instructions (sometimes called a Rubric) on the front of the exam paper, and the head of each section. AND RESOLVE TO FOLLOW THEM!

- ☐ Fill in relevant sections on the front of the paper or answer booklet: eg. your name and/or candidate number.

- ☐ Check for instructions about labelling answer sheets as you go along, or listing the numbers of the sections/questions you have attempted.

- ☐ Check how many questions you must answer, from which sections. Note any questions or sections that are compulsory.

- ☐ Check how long you have for the exam as a whole, and what time it will finish.

- ☐ Check for advice about the timing of sections or questions. (If none is given, work it out from the marks available: see Unit 9.2) If you can, work out the time at which you will need to start each section or question.

- ☐ Check for instructions as to what equipment and resources you are recommended, allowed and not allowed to use in the exam.

- ☐ Check for instructions about how to answer particular types of question.

Go for it!

Look at the specimen exam cover sheet, over the page, and work through our checklist. Underline instructions or information you think are particularly important.

Top tip

On the exam paper, draw a small box in pencil next to each thing you are asked to do. Tick them off as you do them. When they are all done, you could rub them out if you think they look untidy – or leave them as evidence of your organised approach!

THE EXAM PAPER

Fantasy Assessment Board
FAB

General Certificate of Secondary Education

Centre No.
Candidate No.
Surname & initials (Block letters)
Signature
Date

FANTASY STUDIES
Paper 1 (Syllabus X)

Thursday 16 June 199X   9.30am – 11.30am

In addition to this paper you will need:

- Normal writing instruments
- Answer book (provided)
- World map (provided)

Time: 2 hours

Question numbers

Instructions to candidates

- In the boxes above, write your centre number, candidate number, surname and initials, signature and the date.

- This paper is in four sections. Each section covers a different Area of Study.

- Answer THREE questions: ONE from Section A and TWO others, each from a DIFFERENT Area of Study.

- Write your answers in the answer book provided.

- Additional answer sheets will be issued on request. All sheets must be clearly numbered, and fastened securely to the answer book.

- In the column on the right labelled Question Numbers, write the number of EACH question you have answered.

Information for candidates

- This paper is worth 40% of your final award in Fantasy Studies.

- All questions carry 30 marks.

- The marks for the various parts of questions are shown in brackets: eg (2)

- You may bring annotated copies of your texts into the examination room with you, but you must not use any additional notes or materials.

- The use of dictionaries is not allowed in this examination.

- You will be awarded marks for accurate spelling, punctuation and grammar.

- This paper has 12 questions. There is one blank page.

Turn over

THE EXAM PAPER

8.2 Questions, questions!

The most common reason for lost marks is *failing to answer the question*: not the question you wish had been set – but the question the examiner actually wants the answer to! No excuses: the question holds the keys to exactly what's required ...

Topic keys

Key words (and pictures) tell you what the question is about, so you can cover:

- all the topic areas specified and
- only the topic areas specified.

"How has the diet of Eskimos adapted to their environment?"
The topic is 'Eskimos' – but what two things is the question actually about?

Instruction keys

Instruction keys tell you to give your answer in a particular way.
- Circle the correct answer, or cross out the incorrect answer (multiple choice)
- Label items on a diagram/map, or draw a diagram/map
- Complete a sentence
- Write a certain number of lines
- Write in your own words/in modern English/in French/in note form

Instruction keys tell you how many answers are required.
- Name three ... Give three examples of ... What three factors ... ?
- Give other examples of things that (a) do ... and (b) don't ...
  (Think about it – that's a minimum of 4 examples)
- What is the purpose of ... and how is it used? (2 answers required)

Instruction keys tell you what 'angle' to take on the topic.
- **Analyse:** Identify key features and show how they relate or function.
- **Calculate:** Give workings and a numerical solution.
- **Comment:** Give your own thoughts.
- **Compare:** Show how things are similar (+ Relate)
- **Contrast:** Show how things are different (+ Differentiate, Distinguish)
- **Define:** Give the exact meaning of a term.
- **Describe:** Show in detail what happens, or what something is like.
- **Discuss:** Give a balanced view of a subject or statement.
- **Evaluate:** Show good and bad points, and give your judgement (+ Criticise)
- **Explain:** Show reasons or causes (+ Account for) or give the meaning (+ Interpret)
- **Illustrate:** Give examples
- **Justify:** Give reasons and evidence for a view (+ Prove, Demonstrate)
- **Outline:** Give a brief account of the main points (+ Summarise)
- **Suggest:** Offer a solution: there's no 'one right answer'.

Go for it!

'Explain how the diet of the Eskimos has adapted to their environment.'

'Illustrate how the diet of the Eskimos has adapted to their environment.'

'Describe the diet of the Eskimos.'

'Evaluate the diet of the Eskimos.'

What's the difference?

THE EXAM PAPER

8.3 Choosing questions

Do you have a choice?

Don't count on avoiding the topics you don't like altogether! Bear in mind that:

- Some questions may be compulsory.
- You may have to answer a set number of questions from specific sections of the paper.
- Some papers (for example, multiple choice) require you to answer all questions.

Where you can choose, try and do it in a systematic fashion. (The question that just 'catches your eye' is bound to look impossible – and you don't need to spook yourself at this stage …)

Action Checklist

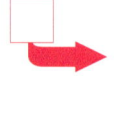

☐ ➤ Read through the entire paper once, carefully. Underline the topic and instruction keywords as you go, so you know exactly what each question requires of you! (If this doesn't ring a bell, see Unit 8.2)

☐ ➤ Write down at the beginning of each section of the paper how many questions (if any) you must answer from it. Check all the instructions, and do this carefully!

☐ ➤ Circle the number of any question that is compulsory. (It's chosen itself!)

☐ ➤ Go back through the other questions a second time. The underlined key words will tell you whether/how well you can tackle each question: put a tick (No Problem), cross (Not Good) or question mark (Not Sure) against each.

> **Hint**
> Don't be put off a question because one part of it is a problem. Check how many marks are available for that part: they may be insignificant compared to the rest of the question, which you could get good marks on.

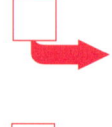

☐ ➤ Select the required number of questions and circle the question numbers. Start with as many 'ticks' as possible, then settle for 'question marks' (which may not be as bad as you think).

☐ ➤ If you have the choice, decide the order in which you'll tackle your ringed questions, and number them.

☐ ➤ Check that you have the right number of questions, drawn from the right sections.

☐ ➤ Start on the question you've numbered '1'!

Top tip

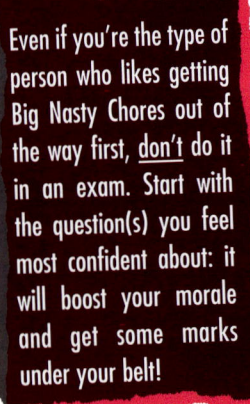

Even if you're the type of person who likes getting Big Nasty Chores out of the way first, <u>don't</u> do it in an exam. Start with the question(s) you feel most confident about: it will boost your morale and get some marks under your belt!

Go for it!

If you haven't already tried it, get hold of a past exam paper and try this checklist!

Where to next?
Unit 9.1: Planning your answers!

ANSWERS!

9.1 Planning answers

Even sentence-completion and two-line answers should be planned – if only in your head. For example: think of a whole sentence before you start it (and find you can't finish it ...) and check that your answer fits the space available. (No extra marks for over-running!)

For slightly longer answers (say 5-10 lines), try jotting down in pencil, in the margin, the keywords of points you need to include, then numbering them in answer order. (Rub all this out when you've finished, for tidiness.)

Why 'waste time' planning an exam essay?
- You get ideas down before you 'lose' them, which boosts your recall – and your confidence, as the marks start adding up.
- You can organise your ideas, with a sense of how the whole answer hangs together.
- A checklist of points will let you work more quickly – without forgetting anything!
- It looks organised, which examiners tend to like ...
- You'll have shown your intentions, in case you run out of time.

As for essay questions...

☐ **Brainstorm.** On a spare sheet of paper, write down relevant points and examples as they occur to you. (If you're used to mind-mapping, do that. See Unit 5.6)

☐ **Number the points**, in a sensible order that suits the question. (Remember your notes, and the underlying patterns of different approaches: Unit 5.3)

☐ Now switch to the answer sheet, and simply list your points neatly and briefly, in order, under appropriate headings and sub-headings.

☐ When you've finished your full answer, put a line through your plan, so that it doesn't distract the examiner – but is legible (if necessary).

So how long ...?
For every half hour you have to spend on a question, allow up to 5 minutes for planning.

Go for it!
The only way to get good at answer planning is to plan answers. So find some questions in a Study Guide or past papers, and have a go!

ANSWERS!

9.2 Timing answers

How much time per question?

The examiner may 'recommend' a time. If not, you can work it out (quickly), using:

- the number of **questions** you have to answer in the time of the exam; and
- the number of **marks** available for each question, as a share of the total.

Example
Exam time: 3 hours
One compulsory question: 40 marks
Plus three questions: 20 marks each

180 mins −10 for reading etc = 170 mins
40 out of 100 marks = $2/5$. $2/5$ of 170 = 68 mins
20 out of 100 = $1/5$. $1/5$ of 170 = 34 mins each

Use the same method for **parts** of a question. If marks aren't given, the question itself ('Name TWO ... ') and the amount of answer space should give you a rough idea.

Top tip

Leave 5–10 minutes out of your calculations. You'll need them at the start of the exam, for analysing questions, and working out timings! And don't forget that within the time for each question, you'll need to allow for planning (Unit 9.1) and checking (Unit 9.5).

Go for it!

How would you allocate your time on the following? (Suggestions below...)
1. Exam time: 2 hours. Questions: 3. Each question carries 30 marks.
2. Exam time: 1 hr, 30 mins. Questions: 30 (multiple choice). All carry equal marks.
3. Question 1: allow 45 mins. 20 marks: (a) 1. (b) 4. (c) 15.

Fitting it all in ...

For a start:

Make sure you can see a clock, or put your watch on the table in front of you.

Work out a start/finish time **for each question you've chosen** and **write it down**.

Timing is hardest with several long questions. You'll be tempted to keep going on those you feel good about: surely a couple of Perfect Answers will make up for the rest? ... No. The first half of the marks available for any question are the easiest to get: the last few marks – which may just edge you into a top grade - are really tough. And you get no marks at all for answers you don't have time to attempt! So here are your real options.

- Finish answers to all the questions required. This takes planning and pruning: stick to main points, with single examples of each. The best option, if you can do it.
- If you find you're running out of time on a question, don't panic. Get as far as you can in the time you planned, then *move on to the next question*. This will get you *most* of the way through *all* the questions: an efficient way of building up marks...
- If you find you're going to be a whole answer short, *still* don't panic! The fall-back option is to draw up an answer plan, and write at least the introductory paragraph of an answer, summarising your argument. It gives the examiner something to go on...

Go for it! suggested answers:
1. 15 minutes planning/checking. 105 minutes ÷ 3 = 35 minutes each.
2. 90 minutes ÷ 30 = 3 minutes each. Allow just under, to save checking time.
3. 5 minutes planning/checking. (a) $1/20$ of 40 minutes = 2 minutes (b) $4/20$ = 8 minutes (c) $15/20$ = 30 minutes.

Exams

9.3 Presenting your answers

Of course, this will entirely depend on the question – and on how you approach it. But here are some general tips for helping (and perhaps even impressing) the examiners ...

Be neat!

If examiners can't follow your workings, interpret your diagrams, read your writing, or work out what comes next in a forest of crossings out, arrows and asterisks – they don't *have* to spend time and effort trying! You want your answer to be read (it's the only way to get marks) and you want to get the examiner on your side. So?

- Write legibly!
- Label diagrams and tables clearly.
- Lay out workings neatly down the page – not all over the place.
- Cross things out with a single straight line: don't scribble!
- Break long passages into chunks of related points: paragraphs or sections.
- Use headings and sub-headings to indicate new topics and topic subdivisions.
- Consider numbering your points, especially if they are in list form.
- Don't overcrowd a page. Leave space between sections, and around diagrams.
- Don't leave gaps, hoping to fill them later. (You won't.) Too obviously desperate!

Go for it!

Look over some of your notes and coursework assignments, with teachers' comments. Which aspects of presentation do you have a problem with? Put a tick or cross against elements in our checklist that you're good or bad at. What are you going to do about it?

Show your workings

In topics which require calculation, it's a good idea to show clearly the procedures you followed to arrive at your answer. Even if you get the *calculation* – and therefore the answer – wrong, you will still be given marks for getting the *method* right!

Q: A 6 volt torch battery delivers a current of 0.5 amps for one hour. How much electrical energy does it provide?

Workings:

$$E \text{ (joules)} = V \text{ (volts)} \times I \text{ (amps)} \times t \text{ (seconds)}$$
[Energy]   [Voltage]   [current]   [time]

Energy = $6 \times 0.5 \times (60 \times 60)$
= 10,800 Joules

Solution: The torch battery provides 10,800 of electrical energy.

ANSWERS!

9.4 Answer tips for question types

Objective ('multiple choice') questions

Multiple choice questions ask you to choose the correct answer from a number of options.

→ Read the questions carefully, considering all the options.
→ Don't spend too long on difficult questions. Move on and come back later.
→ Don't leave questions unanswered: if in doubt, give your best guess.
→ Rule out as many wrong options as you can, to increase your chance of guessing right.
→ Give your answer as instructed. You may be asked to:
  – Delete an incorrect alternative.
  – Choose the correct option from four or five, identified by letter.
  – Link items on one list with matching items on another.
  – Label features on a diagram/map from a list of terms/names.

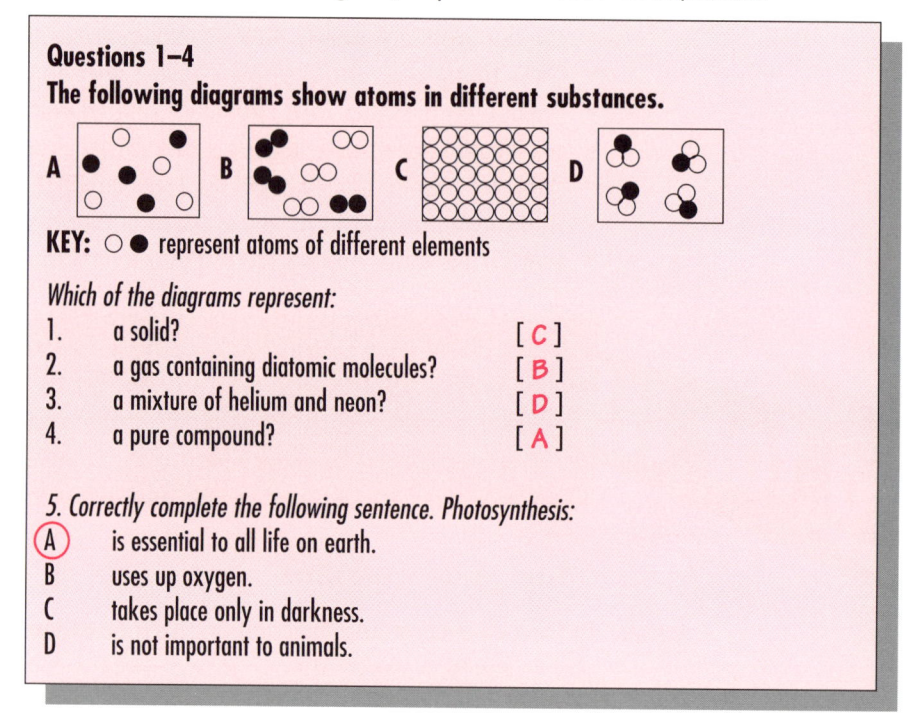

Questions 1–4
The following diagrams show atoms in different substances.

A B C D

KEY: ○ ● represent atoms of different elements

Which of the diagrams represent:
1. a solid? [C]
2. a gas containing diatomic molecules? [B]
3. a mixture of helium and neon? [D]
4. a pure compound? [A]

5. Correctly complete the following sentence. Photosynthesis:
(A) is essential to all life on earth.
B   uses up oxygen.
C   takes place only in darkness.
D   is not important to animals.

Short answer and structured questions

Short-answer questions ask you to come up with your own (brief) answer, in the form of a single word or phrase, a list, a sentence, or the completion or labelling of a diagram.

Structured questions can include short, or more extended, questions. They usually consist of a photo, diagram, table of data or source text, followed by a series of questions. And you usually have to write your answers in space provided in the question/answer booklet.

→ Read the introductory information first, carefully.
→ Read each part of the question carefully: it is usually quite precise.
→ Note the marks available for each part, and allocate space and time accordingly.
→ You needn't fill all the space, but think twice if your answer seems *very* short.
→ If (with average handwriting) your answer overruns the space, you're wasting time on too much detail.

ANSWERS

1. (a) The diagram below shows an elbow joint.

   A _Humerus_
   B _Ligament_
   Cartilage
   C _Synovial fluid_
   D _Ulna_

   (i) Label parts A–D (2)
   (ii) State the function of part B. (1)
   It holds the joint in place.
   (iii) On the diagram, draw and label the cartilage in the correct position. (2)
   (iv) Describe two features of the joint which help it move smoothly. (2)
   The cartilage is smooth and slippery, and the synovial fluid lubricates the joint.
   (v) Explain how the action of pairs of muscles causes the bones to move at the joint. (3)
   The biceps muscle contracts, raising the lower arm, while the triceps muscle relaxes, to allow the movement. The muscles work 'antagonistically' to one another.

Extended prose and essay questions

Such questions ask you to write coherent, continuous text, for anything from 6-10 lines (for a long structured-question part) to as many answer sheets as you like (for an essay). This takes better exam technique than any other question type: remember the following!

➤ Read all questions, and choose carefully (if you have a choice).   See *Unit 8.3*

➤ Carefully allocate – and keep an eye on – your time.   See *Unit 9.2*

➤ Plan any answer over about 2 or 3 sentences.   See *Unit 9.1*

➤ Answer the question, the whole question and nothing but the question!
   See *Unit 8.2*

➤ Start with an introduction and end with a conclusion - however brief.

➤ Break up long answers with paragraphs and headings, for easy reading.

➤ Don't waffle! It wastes time, doesn't gain marks, and annoys examiners.

➤ Don't hesitate to use lists, diagrams, graphs (etc) where appropriate.

➤ Check your spelling, grammar and punctuation.

Name an area in any part of the world where industry has declined. Describe the reasons for the decline and the effects on the people living there. (9)

How successful were the domestic policies of the German government in the years 1933-9? (15)

Choose a character from any TWO of the books you have read for this Area of Study, and contrast their experience of school life. What factors in the personality of the characters contribute to the differences you identify? (20)

ANSWERS!

People

"During the exam, there was no friendliness, no chat at all. It was absolute silence, except you could hear pencils being chewed or what have you. So that made me nervous, and I remember thinking: 'it's only a different room, just a bigger room, don't get into a flap about it' – but I did. The formality changed the way I felt."

"You'd walk up to the exams and it'd be, 'oh no', you know: the thought of turning over a paper and not being able to answer a single question. But it never actually happened."

Going into a big exam is - for me - like going into a big match, like playing for England, or a Newcastle versus Sunderland match. All the stresses are there. People want you to do well... and you want to do well.

Les Ferdinand

Newcastle United and England centre forward.

Exams

58

9.5 Checking your answers

Try and leave yourself:

➡ 2–3 minutes at the end of your time for each long question, or

➡ 5–10 minutes at the end of the exam (especially a multiple choice paper).

> **OK. Let's be realistic. If you're rushing to finish the last question, the last thing you want to do is take time to read back over marks you've already earned!**

BUT ... Checking time is never wasted.

➡ There may be short-answer or multiple choice questions – or aspects of essay questions – that you've accidentally missed out, which you've still got time to answer.

➡ There may be short-answer or multiple choice questions you've *left* out, for later inspiration: now or never!

➡ There may be longer or essay questions that you 'abandoned' for lack of time, which you could go back and finish.

➡ You may have made some careless errors that are immediately obvious when you read over them in the comparative calm of checking time.

➡ Your brain may have run ahead of your pen (or vice versa): sentences that don't make sense are easier to spot when ~~your~~ you're reading than when you're writing.*

➡ You may have brushed over doubtful spellings and punctuation as you wrote your answers: now's the time to go back and try a few alternatives until you feel happier. (Remember: there are marks available for this kind of stuff...)

➡ You may not have completed all the items on your front cover instruction checklist. (The listing of questions answered is particularly easy to forget.) Now is the time!

* If you *do* make corrections or additions to your answers – like this – do it neatly!

Meet the examiner!

Examiners are The Enemy: to beat them, you must outsmart their efforts to trick and destroy you! Sorry: only joking. Actually, examiners are there to help you demonstrate – and get credit for – what you've learned. They're on your side! Want to keep them that way? Here's a few things to think about...

Examiners are human

They even took exams, once upon a time! So they understand about nerves, and time pressure, and little misunderstandings over questions...

> "I once revised for 'A' level European history, and arrived in the exam room to find that it was the English history exam. I learned about proper preparation – the hard way."
> Peter, Chief Examiner, English & English Lit

Examiners want you to do your best

Seriously. Exam papers include lots of instructions and advice to help you answer questions in ways that will win you marks. Look out for them! 1) you deserve all the help you can get, and 2) this is the examiner we're talking about! And there are no 'trick questions': examiners don't get their kicks reading confused or irrelevant answers hour after hour...

> "From an examiner's point of view a 'good question' is one that lets the students know exactly what to do and how to do it. Our only 'trick' is to keep varying the phrasing of questions – so students actually have to read them!"
> Peter

> "We often give advice about the answer: things you 'must' or 'should' include, or things you 'might like to' include – a useful starting point if you're a bit panicky or lost for ideas when you start planning your answer. These guidelines are meant to help you gain marks."
> Peter

Examiners will even give you the benefit of the doubt – given half a chance

Anybody can get a bit lost, or run out of time. Examiners will give you credit where they can – but they can't just assume that you knew what you were doing! Answer plans, introductions and workings give them something to go on...

> "I actually took a Maths exam when I was a boy, in which I got the answer wrong in every single question – but still passed, because I got all the working right!"
> Bob, Chief Examiner, Science

Examiners are only human

Believe it or not, they get tired and fed up – just like you! And they have lots of scripts to mark. Imagine what would get to you if you were an examiner – and AVOID it!...

"Students tend to make the same mistake every year. They look at a question and answer something which is nearly the same – but not the question we're actually asking."
Bob

"I see so little evidence of careful answer planning…"
Peter

Examiners get annoyed if you ignore them or treat them like idiots

"Don't start answering a question before you've read it! The question itself often contains information, which is there to help you. It wouldn't be there unless it was needed – and it's very obvious when it's been ignored!"
Bob

Like when you don't obey their instructions, or answer the question set. It's not just that you're ticking off the person who's marking your paper (Yeah, right. Real smart move.): you won't get any marks either! Don't waste your time…

Examiners have seen it all

Yes. They know waffle when they see it. They know that sneaky sidetrack. That pre-prepared answer. That 'accidental' smudge over an uncertain spelling. Again, don't waste your time…

"I wish I could stop candidates writing out the question at the head of their answers. Perhaps they find it calming, but it is entirely wasted effort, and it only makes one wonder whether they are stalling for time."
Bob

QUIET PLEASE EXAMINER WORKING

ANSWERS!

9.6 In case of emergency...

**SOS!
Sudden Overall Stoppage!**

If you need something ...

Attract the invigilator's attention (silently if at all possible), explain and ask. This applies whether you need to:

- Go to the toilet
- Take medication
- Replace broken equipment
- Get hold of forgotten equipment
- Ask for note paper or extra answer sheets.

Don't ask other exam candidates: the attempt may be misunderstood!

If your mind goes blank ...

➡ Almost all students worry about this. And it almost never happens. Once you're into the business of answering questions, adrenalin and ideas tend to flow. But if you find yourself panicking as you face a new question, or suddenly can't remember something, here are a few things you can do.

➡ Concentrate on the instructions given on the paper, and on your procedures for reading and choosing questions (Units 8.2, 8.3) The feeling that you know what you're doing – and that you're giving yourself the best chance of picking up the basic marks – is pretty reassuring. It also gives you something to be getting on with, instead of worrying.

➡ Focus on the key words in the question you're looking at, and let them trigger your memory of the topic. You might associate a word with other words in your revision notes, or you might be able to visualise it in your diagrams.

➡ Write down each thing that you remember *immediately* on a spare sheet of paper. (Or if you're into mind mapping, do it that way.) It is reassuring to watch the material (and marks) build up, and each note tends to trigger your memory of another.

➡ If you get completely stuck on a particular question, just leave it, and try to find another one that will get you going (and boost your confidence) again. You may well have done enough to pass, already, so take heart.

➡ Don't look around at other people beavering away, or staring into space: it'll only spook you, either way.

➡ If your heart's pounding and you just can't concentrate, try the Slow Deep Breathing exercise (page 13), quietly and briefly.

If someone tries to attract your attention ...

Anyone other than the invigilator is Off Limits during the exam. Don't talk to others, and ignore them if they try to talk to you. Don't accept messages, or pick up things other people drop. If there's a perfectly innocent problem, let them sort it out themselves. You don't have to blow the whistle on would-be cheats, but don't risk your own future!

SO THERE IS LIFE AFTER EXAMS!

10.1 After the exam

However good or bad you feel about it, resist the urge to talk to others about your answers, or how the exam has gone for you. Everybody thinks they've done worse than they really have, and you'll only stress and depress yourself for the next exam – or the wait for results.

Instead, go straight out and do something completely unrelated to school work. The more fun and active, the better: you need to release some tension – and you've deserved it!

Top tip

What you CAN usefully learn from each exam is how to:

- Choose your questions better
- Time your answers better
- Interpret and obey instructions
- Answer new types of question

IF YOU'VE JUST DONE AN EXAM, PUT THIS KIT DOWN AND GO *PLAY!*

10.2 Between exams

Treat the period between exams like the time before your first exam (Units 6.1–6.4). If you plan to revise for the next exam(s), remember: *no* new topics in the last couple of days, and nothing at all the night before.

A lot will depend on how spread out your exams are.

→ If they're far enough apart, try to have a whole day's 'wind down' *after* each exam and *before* the next one.

→ Be especially kind to yourself if you have a very intensive exam schedule, with two exams per day, or more than five in a week. Give yourself loads of food, sleep, fresh air, exercise and treats...

Looking forward ...

Allow yourself to look forward to the end of exams, and the holidays that follow. Obviously, you don't want to waste time day-dreaming, but:

- Keep yourself going, by thinking how great it will feel when you've finished – and passed!
- Console yourself for the things you've 'missed' while revising: you'll be able to do them all, soon – with the added feelgood factor of having done your best in the exams!

Realise that – however badly you feel the exams have gone (and nobody ever seems happy with them) – life goes on, and there are many good things to look forward to.

SO THERE IS LIFE AFTER EXAMS!

10.3 Congratulations: you made it!

Time to party...

Waiting for results

The exams are over, and hopefully you've done OK – or better! But you won't know for a while. And the uncertainty can be pretty nerve-racking. So try and keep things in proportion: (See page 16 ...)

The point is, there's no point loading yourself with worries now: you'll have plenty of time to consider your options when you know how you've actually done.

"I know the run-up to exams is going to curtail my social life really tragically. But there's this huge party afterwards – so I'll just look forward to that!"

"I wasn't expected to do very well, and I said: 'I'll just do what I can do.' And the results were – well, ridiculously good. I'm still sure they're not mine."

"It's a really nice feeling. You feel like you've achieved something – and you have!"